SO-AWA-608

Montana
Behind the Scenes

DURRAE AND JOHN JOHANEK

TWODOT

HELENA,
MONTANA

Dedication

To all our friends and family wherever they might be, and especially to Jamie and Kris, who lost their mother to Montana's wilderness.

A TWODOT BOOK

©2000 Falcon® Publishing, Inc., Helena, Montana.
Printed in the United States of America.

1 2 3 4 5 6 7 8 9 10 BP 05 04 03 02 01 00

All rights reserved, including the right to reproduce any part of this book in any form except for brief quotations for review, without written permission of the publisher.

All photos by the authors unless otherwise credited.
Cover photos by the authors.

Project Editor: Megan Hiller
Production Editor: Jessica Solberg
Text and cover design by Jeff Wincapaw
Page composition by Jeff Wincapaw

Library of Congress Cataloging-in-Publication Data
Johanek, Durrae, 1948–
   Montana behind the scenes / Durrae and John Johanek
     p. cm.
   "A TwoDot Book"--T.p. verso.
   ISBN 1-56044-791-5
   1. Montana--Guidebooks. I. Johanek, John, 1948- II. Title.
 F729.3 .J64 2000
 917.8604'34--dc21

                                         99-086332

For extra copies of this book and information about other TwoDot books, write Falcon, P.O. Box 1718, Helena, MT 59624; or call 1-800-582-2665. You can also visit our website at www.Falcon.com or contact us by e-mail at falcon@falcon.com.

Contents

Acknowledgments

A heartfelt thank you goes out to all the people we met along the way who showed us such wonderful hospitality that we can't wait to go back.

Special thanks to Megan Hiller, who has the patience of a saint, and Arik Ohnstad, who got the ball rolling.

The following people have given time, expertise, and advice. Thank you to Babete Anderson; Burdette Anderson; Ginny Archdale; Karla, Gordon, and Mandi Aus; Rob Ayers; Dennis Berg; Libby Berndt; Larry Bittner; Marlene and Bob Blome; Vicki Braden; Jacque Brett; Mary Cates; Frank Colwell; Joy Day; Bob and Lynn DeArmond; Frank DeRosa; Don and Marla DeShaw; Pat Druckenmiller; Carol Dyke; Chuck Egan; John Ellingson; Patti Erickson; Carol Feddes; Lawrence Flat Lip; Cornelia Flikkema; Jerry Friend; Bob Gardiner; Beulah Hagerman; Shari Hallock; Bill Hanley; Lloyd and Ann Harkins; Bill and Kolene Haun; Ray Heagney; Jim Heck; Dorothy Henderson; Lora Heyen; Rebecca Korell; Jane Lambert; Margo Land; Jeff Landers; Roper Lanier; Patricia Lewis; Betsy Liese; Sylvia Lyndes; Anna Maine; Bob McCurdy; Mary Kay McGrath; Peter McNair; Kim Miske; Missouri River Country; Montana Department of Fish, Wildlife & Parks; Shirley Mouat; Pat Mysse; Lavonne Nemitz; Rita Nemitz; Kathy Nicholson; Ken Oravsky; Earl Osse; Jeanne Parker; Brian Perkins; John Phillips; Pat Pierson; Fritz Prellwitz; Orville Quick; Sharon Rau; Rodger Reynolds; Grace Sanford; Susan Sanford; Dennis Scarnecchia; Sheriff Schatz; Connie Schlievert; Brad Schmitz; Bruce Selyem; Jack Sigman; Shirley Smith; Kathy Steele; Carolyn Steorts; Renee Stoll; Roxie Stroud; Twila Talcott; Mildred Taurman; Beverly Terry; Maxine Thompson; Rod and Lisa Thompson; Vicki Trabold; Ray and Cheryl Trumpower; Verdine White; Warren and Shirley White; Ellen Worth; and Jessi Zeeck.

Introduction

About the State

Montana is the most beautiful state in the country—just ask any Montanan. Although you might get an argument from Idaho or Wyoming, the boast is not an idle one. Montana's also the third largest state—documented fact, no dispute there. At 500 miles by 300 miles, there's lots of diversity: from prairie, cropland, and badlands in the east to forests, mountains, and some of the world's best trout fishing streams in the west. In between is the stark beauty of the Missouri breaks and the high desert of Charlie Russell country. Its badlands are equal to and in many ways surpass those of the Dakotas, without the crowds and commercialism.

Why We Wrote the Book

Some people come to Montana and visit Glacier or Yellowstone National Parks and feel they've seen the state. Some Montanans have lived here all their lives and feel *they've* seen the state, but they haven't experienced what's right over the hill. So, this book is for visitors and locals alike, and although it's not meant to be a travel guide, we hope it will spur you to take your rental car or pickup truck just a little farther down the road. At the very least it should make for good armchair reading and leave you more informed about the state even if you never leave your driveway.

What We Cover

You won't find the obvious here—the parks, resorts, major museums, rodeos, powwows—all the usual touristy stuff. We've looked for the more obscure, less hyped things unique to Montana and tried for a mixture of festivals, unusual museums, nature, history, geology, and a sprinkling of oddities. Many are things you may have driven past without giving a second glance; others you may have noticed and wondered about. *Montana Behind the Scenes* gives you the story behind each one.

It's a big state but we tried to include something from each region. We visited every site, several more than once. Some are funny, some are serious, some can be done as day trips, and some are not meant to be trips at all, but all are pure Montana.

How to Use This Book

In the following 44 chapters there are maps to show you each site's general location in Montana. You can find your way with any Montana highway road map or the *DeLorme Montana Atlas & Gazetteer* (both of which are permanent fixtures in our car). At the end of each chapter are general directions as well as someone to contact for more information, if applicable. Some photos stand alone and need no caption, and "Did You Knows" are sprinkled throughout. The book, like our travels, is completely random and follows no geographical or alphabetical logic, so it's easy to pick up and start reading anywhere. It doesn't get much simpler than that.

Along the Way

We covered more than 12,000 miles, went through every county, crossed the Missouri and Yellowstone Rivers countless times, met hundreds of people, and could have gone for another 12,000 miles—there's still plenty to see. We were constantly amazed how much everything is interconnected in so large an area. For example, we ran into a lot of people who were either from Ekalaka or know someone who lives there—amazing, considering the town has only 200 residents. Then there's Wendy the telephone operator. In trying to find out more about the hay bales in Hobson, we called information and asked the operator (Wendy) to connect us to anyone in Hobson. From her base in Spokane, Wendy said her grandmother lives there and wouldn't mind talking to us, so we were given Grandma's number.

At Crystal Park we ran into some folks who were good friends of Earl Osse, the subject of our second chapter; in Joliet, while walking through the Bible, we were shown the stairway of the steamship *Josephine*, which was described to us on our tour of Pompeys Pillar; and it seemed like everyone has a relative attending Montana State University in our hometown of Bozeman. It made the state seem very small.

Scheduling conflicts surfaced more than once. Sometimes events were scheduled on the same dates, and we had to flip a coin. In one case we agreed to help a fellow move just so he wouldn't cancel our interview.

If You Decide to Go

First, read the gumbo chapter. Then read it again, and memorize it. If it seems like we put a lot of importance on gumbo, we do. It can bog you down and really ruin your day.

Second, if you don't already know it, learn the cowboy wave. Found almost exclusively on dirt roads, there are at least four types, depending on the driver. First is the nearly imperceptible head nod; then there's the single finger slightly lifted off the steering wheel (not to be confused with the less friendly middle-finger wave); next is the modified peace sign, again barely clearing the steering wheel; and finally you have the all-out howdy-glad-to-see-you wave that's usually accompanied by a driver grinning from ear to ear. While styles vary, the most important thing is to make sure you wave back.

Most land appears to be unposted, but pay special attention to gates and fenceposts bearing orange blazes—they mean no trespassing. There are very few sites we visited that required crossing private land, and it's common courtesy to respect landowners' rights. If you have any doubts, ask first.

Whenever you can, park the car and walk, whether out on the prairie or in downtown Butte—smell the sage, aspen, and pine; listen to the howl of coyotes and *hootle* of sandhill cranes; discover interesting architecture or a unique backyard garden.

Enjoy the wildlife from a safe and sane distance, whether birds or bears. And no matter how cute they are or how much they beg, do not feed them—it could cost them their lives. Keep an eye out for grizzlies (not a big problem in Butte) and when in rattlesnake country, watch where you put your hands and feet. Above all, always follow a zero-impact policy.

Part of the adventure is getting there, and remember, Montana does have a speed limit. Be prepared for any kind of weather; it changes quickly and can vary greatly. It's wise to call ahead to confirm hours of operation or road conditions. Don't drive long stretches nonstop—sometimes the state's beauty can lull you to sleep. To make our trips a little more interesting and relaxing, we pack a set of horseshoes—that's right, horseshoes. Nearly every park in every town, no matter how small, has horseshoe pits free for the using—a nice break on a long trip.

Montana has some great history—stories we heard as kids and paid attention to as adults. In school we learned about Sacagawea, Lewis and Clark, Chief Joseph, even the gang at Robber's Roost, and although reading about them is fine, it means so much more if you visit the sites. Get out and become a part of history.

About the People

Montana was built on mining, logging, and ranching, but the people are its foundation, tough, hardworking folks who have spirit, a sense of humor, and genuine niceness, some of the friendliest in the country. If you get stuck or lost, just wait a few minutes; someone will stop to help you, and it's likely to be a local.

This book is about locations, but it's as much about the people who make up these locations—from the Native Americans who inhabited the ice caves to Orville Quick and his cement brontosaurus. Throughout the state everyone you talk to will tell you they're proud of who they are, where they live, and their heritage. You'll see it in the cowboy wave on a back road. You'll feel it when you listen to them talk about their hometowns. You'll sense it in their sincerity.

Is this the real Montana? You bet.

A Few Words *about* **Gumbo**

Montanans are a hardy breed—from the pioneers who settled here to the loggers, miners, and ranchers. We laugh at minus 30 degrees and chuckle at rattlesnakes. We've even weathered the militia and that fellow in Lincoln. But there's one thing that will stop any Montanan in his tracks and strike fear in his heart—gumbo.

Gumbo is the geological equivalent of—actually, there is no equivalent. It's superfine, powdery silt that was once the bottom of a huge inland ocean, but when you're 50 miles from nowhere and stuck up to your door handles, you don't really give a rat's ass where it came from or how it got there.

East of the divide is where it lies in wait, looking innocently enough like any ordinary dirt road, but just let a few drops of rain soak in and it gets downright mean, making a mockery of four-wheel-drive anything. Feeling smug with your cell phone? Gumbo has swallowed up whole tow trucks that came to "rescue" its victims.

Some of our country's most famous disappearances can be attributed to the vile ooze: Jimmy Hoffa, leisure suits, and eight-track tapes—they're all buried in gumbo. It can't be photographed—it leaves no reflection in a mirror.

Even the state can't bring itself to use the word; it uses euphemisms instead like "road impassable when wet"—the government has a gift for understatement. Choose to ignore the warning, and you'll pay dearly. As you sit there spinning all four wheels, you'll find that it's not only the sun that sinks slowly in the West.

Directions:
None; it will find you.

For more information:
Few have survived it, and those who have refuse to speak of it.

Scene Along the Way

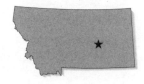

The Woodpeckers *of* **Ryegate**

You've been driving the same section of U.S. Highway 12 nearly every day for the past five years. One day your eye catches a woodpecker perched on a tree, then another, and another. In a few weeks they've multiplied and seem to be everywhere—now you really take notice but still have no clue what they are and why they're there.

The 30 miles of road between Ryegate and Harlowton host 42—give or take a few—red-headed woodpeckers. But before you grab your binoculars and plan a weekend birding trip to see this phenomenon, be forewarned: each one is made of plywood. In Ryegate there's a large handscrawled sign that reads "Woodpecker Crossing Next 30 Miles"—strange enough. But as you head west you can't help but notice these wooden lawn-ornament-like woodpeckers on poles, outbuildings, fenceposts, houses, and just about anywhere they can be attached—stranger yet. Stop in at the store in Ryegate or Shawmut and the darn things are for sale. What gives?

While trying to beautify this stretch of highway, Earl Osse (pronounced O-see) and his friend Jerry Gantz have certainly made it more interesting, Earl being the instigator. Earl is a retired mail carrier and carpenter who describes himself as an almost native, having moved to Ryegate from Jamestown, North Dakota, in 1936. For the past four years he and Jerry have been cutting and hanging woodpeckers—1,500 at last count. "I thought woodpeckers were pretty, and a local teacher suggested I make and hang some. Over the years I made 400 or 500 little ones, but they were stolen faster than we could put them up. If a woodpecker thief couldn't reach his quarry, he would lasso one to pull it down. So we made them bigger and hung them higher—not foolproof, but it has slowed down theft a bit. We even put out a reward, but no luck—never found the culprit."

His first birds were attached to utility poles, which Montana Power

Earl poses in his workshop with a flock of finished roadside wannabes (he gets 25 birds out of one sheet of plywood).

frowned upon and made him take them down, "so we put them in the trees," he says. More than one parent has hailed his cutouts to be responsible for entertaining their kids on an otherwise monotonous drive. "The parents make a game out of counting the woodpeckers—I think they like them as much as the kids do, if just for the peace and quiet in the car."

A dynamic seventy-two years old, Earl's energy is amazing, but even more amazing is the fact that he does all his cutting and hanging with one hand. He lost the use of his arm in a coal mining accident in Roundup when he was nineteen; Jerry has become his second arm. An artistic friend in town got them started with the painting, which they now do themselves. "I like the colors. The bright red and black and white really catch your eye," Earl comments.

Earl and his birds have been featured on television and in regional magazines. He's flattered but shakes his head at his fame and finds it amusing that although he sells the large birds locally for $10, at an estate auction one went for $20. "Must have been a real good friend who bought that one," he chuckles.

From a town of about 300 ("if everyone's home," according to Earl) the birds have found perches all over the country. "I have them in at least thirty-two states. I keep a map that I color in when I find out where my latest sale is going. Most of them range from Alaska through the West and South, with several eastern states accounted for." Some of them have gone international, roosting in Switzerland, Germany, and Canada. A local woman whose husband was working in Russia told Earl of an article from *Montana* magazine posted on the bulletin board in the embassy in Moscow about Earl's birds.

How much longer will Earl be the birdman of Ryegate? "As long as I can," he says. "As long as people enjoy them."

★ *Directions:*
Ryegate is on U.S. Highway 12 midway between Harlowton and Roundup.

did you know...

Montana's entire population is approximately 100,000 less than that of Phoenix, Arizona.

Dutch Dinner, **Churchill**

Does the thought of snert make you salivate? Do you dream about butter-drenched klont? Well, if Cornelia Flikkema invites you to dinner, be prepared to stand in line. You'll be one of the thousand or so who show up for the Dutch dinner—the social event of the year in the Dutch town of Churchill.

Up until 1980 Cornelia ran a coffee shop across the street, where she served a different Dutch specialty every day. When she closed shop, the Manhattan Christian School asked her to host a fundraising supper. Optimistically, Cornelia prepared food for 400 people—600 showed up. Each year she makes more food and each year more people come.

But the dinner is a true community event: volunteers from Churchill and nearby Amsterdam donate all their time and the majority of the food. One local raises the peas, another the kale, and still another provides rutabagas. Even the retirement home gets into the act by peeling the tons of potatoes that go into the Dutch delicacy of stamppot.

Although the last Friday in March (or any Friday in March) in Montana seems like a sure way to get your event canceled due to weather, in farming towns like Churchill it makes sense. This is near the beginning of the planting season in prime potato country—any later and there would be no volunteers.

As you can imagine, for a dinner party this large you'll need a dining room the size of a gymnasium. Guess what—the meal is served cafeteria style in the school gym with four stations, each offering a different specialty. Going Dutch will cost you $7, for which you get a printed menu and a tray and all the roggebrood you can eat. The main course is stamppot—four globs of mashed potatoes flavored with the vegetables they were boiled with—kale, rutabaga, cabbage, and carrots. But to do it up right, you need to dip into the crockpot on the table and douse your potato piles with a ladle full of bacon fat and bits. Sounds awful but it's to die for—really.

Come as you are, come early, and wear loose clothes. The meal is only half the fun—the klompen dancers are a real Dutch treat.

And what's a meal without entertainment? Throughout the dinner kids dressed in Dutch costume, complete with wooden shoes, perform folk dances on the wooden stage. If it weren't for the volume of these klompen dancers, you could probably hear your arteries explode. Carol Feddes, Cornelia's daughter, recalls the year that—gasp—there were no klompen dancers. Public outcry has brought them back.

As you down that last spoonful of grauwe erwten, you wonder how anyone could survive long enough to host the dinner from year to year. Rest assured that few, if any, locals actually make this their regular diet.

Before the poffert settles, loosen your belt and waddle over to the dessert table, the school's real cash cow. Desserts are à la carte and with good reason—you won't be able to stop at just one (hey, it's only once a year). Take a seat on the bleachers and enjoy the crowd and notice that, amazingly, almost no one is overweight.

In twenty years the menu hasn't changed, but who's complaining? The dinner still draws folks from the four corners of Montana as well as many out-of-staters. One year campers at an RV convention in nearby Bozeman got wind of the dinner—attendance soared. Still, Cornelia and the rest of the organizers sometimes wonder if the dinner will remain popular. Will attendance slump? Will people get tired of the same menu? Clearly the answer is, fat chance.

No, wait—the klompen dancers are only half the fun. The desserts are the real Dutch treat.

★ *Directions:*
South of Interstate 90 at the Manhattan exit, in Churchill.

For more information:
406-282-7261; last Friday of March; 4 to 7:30 P.M.

CHURCHILL DUTCH DINNER MENU
(the menu is the same every year)

SOUPS
Kippen Soep *(chicken soup)*
Snert *(split pea soup)*
Served with Roggebrood: dark quickbread covered with shredded
    kaas *(cheese)*

MAIN DISHES
Pot Eten *(aka stamppot)*: whipped potatoes mixed with either kale,
    rutabaga, cabbage, or carrot and perhaps some ham or sausage
Saucijzebroodjes: pigs in a blanket

SPECIALTY DISHES
Klont: steamed buckwheat pudding served hot with bacon drip
    pings, brown sugar, melted butter, or syrup
Poffert: quickbread with bacon served with sweet white sauce
Grauwe Erwten: large dark peas served with bacon topped with
    Dutch mustard or syrup

DESSERT BRIJS
Zoepen Brij: buttermillk soup with cooked barley served with sugar,
    syrup, or honey
Krentje Brij: raisin or currant soup with cooked barley, sugar, and
    raspberries

BAKERY TABLE (a partial list)
Amandel Taartjes *(almond tarts)*, Kringler *(cream puff)*, Blader Deeg
    Gabakje *(almond puff pastry)*, Booke Potjes *(goat's feet chocolate
    cookies)*, Bitter Koekje *(macaroons)*

Greycliff Prairie Dog Town State Park

reycliff prairie dog town by definition qualifies as a real town: it has neighborhoods, residents, a social structure, and even crime, but this hamlet's population consists of rodents—cute rodents to many, pests to ranchers. These denizens, black-tailed prairie dogs, are often mistaken for their relative, the ground squirrel (referred to as gophers almost statewide, which they are not), but there is a difference. The problem lies in telling them apart. To begin with, experts will tell you a prairie dog is bigger, but bigger than what, if you have nothing to compare them with. Also the dog is colonial—again a wonderful identifier if you happen to see a colony of them. Third, prairie dogs are basically vegetarians, and here's where it gets easier to tell one from another. Ground squirrels are omnivorous; the thunk of a car's wheels is like a dinner bell to a ground squirrel, who sees his squished pal as the next meal—a dead giveaway that this is probably not a prairie dog, who is a bit more civilized and feeds on roots and stems.

Although there are many towns across central and eastern Montana, Greycliff has the most accessible and easily viewed residents, who seem oblivious to the semis on the interstate just a few feet from their colony. But depending on the time of year, the lifeless bodies of an unlucky few line the roadway like fuzzy speed bumps. There are plenty of survivors, however. Pull up to an active mound, and they will disappear, but within a few minutes their curiosity wins out, giving the dog watcher great photo ops. Like humans, they're more active in warm, not too hot, weather, although a few diehards can be seen in winter, especially on sunny days.

The black-tailed prairie dog *(Cynomys ludovicianus)* is native and unique to North America and colonizes primarily grazing lands from Canada to the Southwest. Sometimes their numbers get out of hand and

*These camels of the prairie are believed to metabolize their own urine and survive for long
periods on the moisture they get from plants—they do not drink from standing water.*
Photo courtesy of Montana Department of Fish, Wildlife & Parks.

they need to be artificially controlled if they become a nuisance to live-stock—it's not unheard of for livestock to break a leg in a dog hole.

Whether you are friend or foe of these critters, it's impossible to deny their role in the ecosystem they occupy. So many other animals depend on prairie dogs for food and shelter that if the dogs were to disappear it would be devastating to other species' populations. Eagles, ferruginous hawks, foxes, and black-footed ferrets relish and often survive on a tasty dog, whereas burrowing owls, badgers, and rattlesnakes frequently move into abandoned burrows. The mountain plover uses the town's gravelly habitat for nesting.

The town's social system is pretty impressive. The smallest order is the burrow, the individual home. Like most middle-class homes, bur-rows differ from each other: some have a fan shape that indicates it was enlarged by a badger, although the usual prairie style is that of several stories or levels—up to fourteen feet deep. The uppermost level is the listening post, where the watch dog hides when danger threatens and listens to make sure it's safe to go topside again. Below this is the toilet room, and then the dry room, which is used if the lowest level, the cham-ber, is flooded.

Each burrow has a mound of dirt surrounding it that serves as a handy watch post. Like the different burrow styles, mounds vary too—crater-shaped mounds are usually the back door, and dome shapes indicate the front way in. Although only two feet high at the most, a mound must seem like a rooftop to a height-challenged prairie dog. It's from here the guard dog watches for danger. A soaring golden eagle, for example, will cause him to go into action: he twitches his tail and signals the others in town with a series of high-pitched "barks," earning the species its name. The mounds also help keep out high water.

Mounds and burrows comprise coteries, or neighborhoods, that house one or two adult males and two to four females and their young—an extended family. The rules here are strict: no dog may stray into another's coterie or it will be chased away. The average litter of pups is about five, but as many as ten can show their heads aboveground in late spring.

Greycliff is the labor of love for Livingston wildlife photographer Edward Boehm, who was instrumental in preserving the site when the interstate was built here. Assisting was The Nature Conservancy, the Montana Department of Highways, and Fish, Wildlife & Parks. As at any of Montana's state parks, signs warn you to keep your pets on a leash, which is especially important here because prairie dogs carry fleas, which in turn transmit plague—not a serious problem, but why take the chance (plague nearly wiped out a colony at the Charles M. Russell National Wildlife Refuge but the population is recovering). Besides, loose dogs harass wildlife and ruin the experience for others. *Please obey the signs that ask you to not feed the prairie dogs!* No matter how cute or hungry they appear, people food wreaks havoc with their digestive systems and habituates them to humans, making them less wild and a threat to people as well as to their own populations. Your good intentions could kill them, and goodness knows they've already got their hands full with the semis.

★ *Directions:*
Off Interstate 90 about 7 miles east of Big Timber.

For more information:
Montana Department of Fish, Wildlife & Parks, 406-247-2940.

Medicine Rocks State Park,
Ekalaka

Medicine Rocks State Park is aptly named—it's medicine for the soul. The quiet here is almost as unnatural as the rock outcroppings; the only sounds are often the wind and buzzing nighthawks. Jutting out of the surrounding prairie are sandstone pillars, caves, and spires (some eighty feet tall) resembling pockmarked sand castles that have seen one wave too many. They are the remains of feeder streams to the inland sea that covered this area millions of years ago.

Native Americans revered this landscape and came here to get good medicine for a successful hunt. It's said that Sitting Bull and his men summoned the rocks' spirits before the Battle of the Little Bighorn. Young Indian boys would spend three days among these windswept towers on a vision quest: whatever vision they had would become their adult name.

In the late 1800s Theodore Roosevelt camped at Medicine Rocks. He was so impressed with the formations that he carved his name in them— little did he realize the precedent he had set. In spite of rules prohibiting defacing the rocks, inscriptions are everywhere. Teddy's name has faded, but it will take hundreds of years, if ever, for wind and rain to erase the damage from modern-day vandals.

The square-mile park has primitive campsites, hiking trails, picnic facilities, and the best well water for miles around. Once home to herds of elk, bison, and bighorn sheep, today's residents include deer, pronghorn, badgers, bats, and prairie rattlesnakes, but the unseen inhabitants are the spirits—the medicine of Medicine Rocks.

★ *Directions:*
25 miles south of Baker on Montana Highway 7.

For more information:
Montana Department of Fish, Wildlife & Parks, 406-232-0900.

Unlike anything else for hundreds of miles, it's no wonder the Native Americans considered this a special place for good medicine and spiritual renewal.

Granrud's Lefse Shack,
Opheim

It's said that you can get Norwegians to eat fenceposts if you can figure out how to put enough butter on them. But why waste perfectly good butter on a fencepost when you've got lefse? For anyone who's never spent the holidays with a Viking, lefse is a special treat that resembles a crepe or thin tortilla, and no self-respecting Norse table spread would be complete without it. Although it's a Scandinavian thing, it's more closely associated with the Norwegians. So what's this got to do with Montana? In the hamlet of Opheim, just ten miles from the Canadian border, lefse is made literally by the tons. Each week beginning in fall, butter, sugar, and cream—practically the three Scandinavian basic food groups—are used in copious amounts. But the star ingredient is potatoes—63,000 pounds a year.

It all started in 1977 when Myrt Granrud and her neighbor Arlene Larson made a batch for the church's lutefisk* dinner. Commonly eaten with lots of butter and brown sugar, the lefse was a hit—so much so that a friend asked for some to put in her shop in Glasgow. Pretty soon demand exceeded output, and Myrt's husband, Evan, was roped into helping roll them out. And, according to Myrt, they *had* to be rolled, not pressed—it makes a difference in the taste. Whether it was his tinkering nature or his dislike for rolling them, Evan devised a machine to take over this chore. What began as a two-rolling-pin operation, today employs fifteen full-time seasonal lefse makers (fourteen women, one man).

Shari Hallock, savvy manager of the operation, was the Granruds' first employee and has become the spokesperson for Evan and Myrt's lefse since they retired. Frequently her tours for student and senior groups are seasoned with stories of Evan's constant attempts to improve the production process. She'll tell you how the lefse was cooled on a low-tech contraption of two sawhorses and a door. In the days preceding the shack's freezer, it was stored on a pie rack in an unheated breezeway—her first uniform consisted of earmuffs and gloves.

Today the whole process is automated but has taken on a Willy Wonka–like appearance. Wads of the lefse mixture are fed through a device resembling a ringer washer that uses paint rollers and surgical-mesh-covered PVC pipe to roll them so thin you can almost see through them. Evan turned the pipe on a lathe to give it grooves for texturing the lefse, just like hand rolled. To get uniform-size chunks of the raw lefse, he concocted tubes that are stuffed with the dough, which is then cut off at the top with guitar wire. The dough balls then make their way to rolling tables covered with nightgown flannel and floured with Evan's automated sifter.

Here's where the Lefse Ladies come in wielding their favorite lefse sticks to transfer the thin product to the griddle where it cooks at 500 degrees F; the same sticks then put them on the cooling table. Shari says that each woman has her own technique and is particular about the type of stick she uses. To cool down, each lefse must make the trip through a stack of six mesh conveyors, another of Evan's creations that needs to be seen to be appreciated. The product goes to the cutters and is packaged before being taken to the freezer where it awaits shipment to lefse-deprived Norwegians throughout the country. Employees work an eight-hour day, and with overtime during the hectic season it's not unusual for a passing car to see lights on late into the night.

Shari says, "One thing that really sets us apart from other brands is that we use real potatoes instead of flakes," which keeps one farmer in Dagmar very happy. Granrud lefse calls for a combination of red and white potatoes—red for flavor, white for consistency and to keep the mixture dry enough to cook. Evan didn't like peeling potatoes any more than rolling the dough, especially when it meant 1,200 pounds of spuds a day; thus was born his potato peeler that uses a coarse sanding disk to do the job.

Then the things needed to be cooked, so again he tinkered, this time with pressure cookers, and installed pressure release valves at the bases of the pots so they could drain and cool down quicker. From here the potatoes go to Evan's custom-made potato masher, which includes a counterweight hook to lift and hold the heavy beater so it can be scraped clean.

In spite of its remote location, Granrud's Lefse Shack has its share of drop-in traffic, but it's a small percent of their business. At $5 per 1-pound package it's a luxury item for many of the locals. But with regular exposure at events like the Norsk Høstfest in Minot, North Dakota, which draws 60,000 people a day, the demand increases yearly; unfortunately

Because Evan makes so much of this equipment from everyday items like guitar string, paint rollers, and PVC pipe, when something breaks down he can repair it simply by going to the local hardware store.

so do the costs of making it (even with all the mechanization, it's still labor intensive). What makes this lefse so popular, according to Shari, "is our recipe [a closely guarded secret], real potatoes, and rolling instead of pressing, which some people insist makes all the difference in the world."

Norwegian food has the reputation for being bland and white, and lefse is no exception, but not all is created equally. Some is soft, some sweet, some isn't even made with potatoes—Uff Da†; then there's the pressed versus rolled controversy. Although it doesn't have a distinctive flavor and it's not too pretty to look at, lefse's appeal lies in its nostalgia. Shari says that Scandinavians are known for keeping their emotions in check, but not when there's lefse around. To a Norwegian, it's home, it's comfort food, it's like Grandma used to make.

*Lutefisk has no description; you have to be born to it.
†Uff Da is a way of expressing yourself without swearing.

★ *Directions:*
Northeast Montana, 49 miles north of Glasgow on Montana Highway 24.

For more information:
Granrud's Lefse Shack, 406-762-3250.

Lloyd Harkins, **Silver Star**

I f you were around in 1969 you probably remember where you were when Neil Armstrong walked on the moon. Lloyd Harkins knows exactly where *he* was—hauling home a steam shovel that was used to build the Panama Canal. Home for Lloyd is Silver Star, the third oldest town in Montana, named after, oddly enough, a gold mine. Typical of so many mining towns in the West, Silver Star's population has dwindled from its peak of 2,000 to a mere 40, but mining's loss has been Lloyd's gain.

Anyone passing through Silver Star can't miss Lloyd's place, not because of the chain-link fence that surrounds his seven acres but because of what's locked inside it. Mining stuff—literally tons and tons of it—that he has collected over the past forty years. Lloyd was a miner for twenty- five years, and it shows (talk about taking your work home with you). He worked in the Broadway and Melrose mines as well as the Green Camel, the oldest mine in Montana, begun in 1867.

Most of Lloyd's mining equipment is from Butte, but he gets it wherever he can. At seventy-five he feels there's not much left to buy—what's out there is too expensive, so his focus is on restoration. Not officially on public display (only roadside viewing is allowed), many of the thousands of objects are in various stages of repair and he has plans for each one of them, although he agrees that he'd have to live to be 165 to do it all.

At its peak Butte had 138 operating mines—a chunk of them are now in Lloyd's backyard. He managed to haul away just about everything except the 4,000 miles of tunnels that still lie under the city. Boilers, pumps, blowers, trucks, gas pumps, ore cars, steel buckets, railroad cars, pulleys, and a machine that makes corrugated tin roofing—the list is endless. He knows the story behind each object—where it came from, when he bought it, and the problems he had moving it. He knows too what it was for and how it was used. And after decades of tinkering, he certainly knows how it comes apart and goes back together.

Believing that a mine is a terrible thing to waste, Lloyd has donated tons of memorabilia to Butte's World Museum of Mining, but the Gray Rock mine head frame remains as a focal point of Silver Star. He does nearly all the hauling, assembly, and restoration himself.

Towering over this metallic menagerie is a seventy-eight-foot head frame that was used to raise and lower the cages of workers into the mine shaft at Butte's Gray Rock mine. Lloyd took the head frame apart there and brought it back to Silver Star in 1972 but purposely waited to reassemble it until 1982—exactly 100 years after it was built. Waiting to be assembled is a sheav wheel, which was part of another headframe used to haul bodies up from the Speculator mine in Butte, site of the country's worst mining disaster. On the other end of the yard is a timber from yet another head frame that measures two feet square by ninety-one feet long—all one solid piece of wood—from Washington State. After almost 100 years of exposure it's still as straight as when it was cut.

Next to the head frame are the cages, one a two-deck version that could hold sixty-four men. Harkins says, "Things got nasty on that one— the men played jokes on each other and the ones in the lower level got dirt and such dropped on them." Miners were testy after a day's work and fights would often break out.

Wheels are everywhere—pulleys, gears, and spools—but none are more prominent than the five behemoths near the highway. These Silver Star landmarks from the Leonard mine in Butte pumped high-pressure air into the mine for drilling. Nearby stands a fifteen-foot-high blower that ventilated the mines. But Lloyd looks beyond this at an eighty-four-ton

One of the five twenty-one-foot wheels that line Route 41. When Lloyd created this
landmark he had visions of starting a mining museum but decided it would tie him down.
He still buys, sells, and trades in a big way—not much is less than a ton.

wheel that was part of a mine hoist—"the worst thing I ever moved," he says. It was located in a backfilled dump area and the machinery to move it kept sinking every time they tried to lift it out.

Inside a shed—more wheels, wooden patterns for making metal gears. The pattern was pressed into sand and then hot metal was poured into the indentation. Mines had to be self-sufficient, and as a result most had their own blacksmith shops, most of which have ended up in Lloyd's backyard too. What couldn't be made in a mold was forged out of steel. Rods, levers, hooks, handles—all had their day on the anvil. From a 500-pound anvil to a 5-ton press, none is more impressive than the 12-ton swedge block that was used to bend rods into shapes.

Blacksmithing is second nature to Lloyd. One of his must-do projects involves making cowcatchers for two locomotives that were badly burned in a roundhouse fire in Nevada City. When finished they will be displayed at Lloyd's along with his other railroad memorabilia.

But not everything on the property is mining related—if it was a good deal, it became Lloyd's. That's why scattered in this mining maze you'll find a cast-off cemetery headstone, a cast-iron cookstove, and a steel door that came from the vault in copper king Marcus Daly's bank in Butte. The ornate door is so heavy that two men couldn't lift one corner of it when it was lying flat.

Tractor trailers, RVs, locals, and tourists drive past here every day, but when Walt Disney's set designers saw Lloyd's place they pulled in . . . and left with eight semis loaded with stuff. Destination: Euro-Disney's Thunder Mountain ride and Frontier Land. This isn't Lloyd's only contribution to the folks from Anaheim—his artifacts adorn the Indiana Jones ride in Disneyland. If you can't get to France or California, rent the movies *Flood*, *Mouse Hunt*, or Kevin Kostner's *The Postman*—ambience by Lloyd.

More than a collector, Lloyd is a restorer and a damn good one. He has two restored train cabooses to prove it. One is from the Great Northern and the other is from the Union Pacific, which he hauled from Idaho where it had been used as a bunkhouse. He cut four feet off the top to get under the overpasses on the highway, then skillfully riveted it back on and refurbished the entire thing. They both sit in front of his house on rails.

With each restoration comes the preservation of history. Take, for example, the Panama Canal steam shovel. As Lloyd will tell you, it was one of 130 such shovels manufactured by Bucyrus to dig the canal. When the waterway was finished the shovels were sold. This one was purchased by the cement company in Trident fifty miles northeast of here. When

In Lloyd's magic kingdom he turns rusty boilers into decorative pieces like this one that did not make it to Euro-Disney with its siblings. Disney's eight tractor trailers could hold only so much. As a result it stands as one of the few finished projects in the yard.

they no longer needed it Lloyd came to the rescue, and it now sits in his lot covered in years of gray cement dust awaiting its place in history. It has plenty of company.

★ Directions:
17 miles south of Whitehall, exit off Interstate 90 on Montana Highway 55.

Scene Along the Way

Powder River Historical Society
and Mac's Museums, **Broadus**

I f you want to visit the town of Ridge, Montana, you'll have to go to the museum in Broadus—Ridge is in one of the back rooms. Or are you looking for Native American artifacts? They're here too. Cowboy lore? Yup. Arrowheads? Birds' eggs? Butterflies? Uh huh. Rattlesnake rattles? You bet.

All this and more can be found in the Powder River Historical Society Museum, housed in the buildings and bays of a former lumberyard. Horace Broaddus, son of the town's founders (the United States Postal Service screwed up and dropped one "d"), bought the museum building and donated it. Opened in 1988, the museum is operated entirely by volunteers with no county tax support and grows through continual donations and loans of historical items.

On any given day Twila Talcott—one of the more active senior volunteers—may be on duty to give you a personal tour. Although any one of the many high school students are qualified to do the same, Twila can tell you the personal significance of her father's barber pole, one of several family pieces on display. Or Don Heidel—another passionate senior— will proudly point out a patchwork quilt made of his father's neckties. They and other volunteers can recall a story behind almost every memento. For example, the medical doctor's bag fully equipped with gear is nostalgic because everyone had one since they all lived so far from medical care.

Two standouts of local folk art are the friendship quilt made in 1928 and signed by all who worked on it and the hand-carved stagecoach and four horses created by Stanley Damm. But the museum is chockfull of local history, ranging from a mess box on a chuck wagon (with servings for ten) and an unusual Mission-style recliner to the first drum used by the high school band in 1938.

Bob McCurdy and Twila Talcott are living evidence that the museum is evolving. On forays to Twila's ranch, Bob and a friend unearthed a cannon wheel and bullets, remnants of the 1865 Cole expedition from Nebraska. Look for their discoveries when you visit the museum.

But this only hints at what's to come. Open the back door and you'll find Ridge—at least a reconstruction of the town's store (which *was* the town) complete with many of its artifacts, including a gun purchased in 1916. Ridge bit the dust in 1960.

Across the room is the museum's recently acquired spur collection—one of the finest in the state. Step outside for yet another blast from the past. This is the lumberyard proper, which now houses the museum's larger pieces, among them a working still, model A cars, a functioning sheep wagon, and a homesteader's windmill. And if you've ever had a hankerin' to be an Old West sheriff, you can fantasize in the Powder River Jail, complete with cells that were used from 1919 to 1980. Next door you can't miss the steel and wooden steam shovel, which was brought by train to Ekalaka from Minneapolis and from there "walked" at a snail's pace down the dirt roads to Broadus to mine coal and gravel near town.

As you lumber through the yard you might be thinking you've seen it all, but there's more—lots more, namely Mac's Museum, which occupies 1,000 square feet in a low-slung, off-white building in a corner of the yard. One of the town's more colorful residents was Mac McCurdy, so well known by his nickname that his son, Bob, was fifteen before he found out his father's real name was Ralph. Today Bob, seventy, is another ardent museum volunteer, his passion focusing on his father's collections. The senior McCurdy (1889 to 1986) was a unique Broadusonian—so too were his oddball collections. Mac's museum was part of the McCurdy living room for many years until the historical society incorporated it into the complex.

Mac considered himself a honyokker, a derogatory term for a homesteader who had dreams but never more than a few dollars to his name, although he did teach school among other odd jobs. But mainly he was a collector's collector.

Take, for example, his seashells—all 22,000 of them and counting, each one cataloged and labeled. He got his first shells in Dover, Delaware. As county clerk recorder he was a great letter writer and through his writing got in touch with a leper from the Philippines; he pretty much supported the man through his shell buying. He would send him $20 for a huge box of shells, but that fizzled out when he began to get duplicates. Son Bob sent him some from Korea, and Mac began collecting in earnest in 1956, traveling to Sanibel Island in Florida. He arranged to buy bushel baskets of shell-laden sand from Florida for $6 (plus $19 freight), but those too began to duplicate. The result of his efforts is the largest inland shell collection in the country, with shells from nearly every ocean and sea in the world. The smallest shell fits on the head of a pin and the largest—the *Megalatractus proboscidifera* from Australia—is about fifteen inches long.

If seashells aren't your cup of sand, maybe artillery shells are; everything from a .22 to a 90 mm army artillery shell is on display. The mineral collection rivals that of almost any mining museum—2,200 of them as painstakingly labeled and cataloged as the seashells. This includes a few that are tagged "just plain glass" because they came from the glass factory that burned down in Lovell, Wyoming. The 1,720 handsomely mounted arrowheads come from every state in the union. But don't overlook the other Native American objects and collections of birds' eggs, butterflies, and Far Eastern memorabilia.

Today Broadus has a population of about 420; at its peak in 1966 it was triple that when oil was discovered 25 miles away. That oil is now tapped out. When the oil dried up so did the town, but not its spirit, which is why, according to its welcome sign, it's still the "Wavingest Town in the West." And it is.

★ *Directions:*

In southeast Montana at the intersection of U.S. Highway 212 and Montana Highway 59.

For more information:

406-436-2276; open Memorial Day to Labor Day or by appointment; 9 A.M. to 5 P.M. Monday through Saturday. Admission to both museums is free but donations are welcomed.

Cement Art, **Plains**

I f you drive past Bill Haun's place, you'll know it. You can tell by the tree full of vultures, the chipmunks, pigs, bunnies, frogs, ducks, cows, and dogs. And if you were anywhere else but Bill's yard, you'd have to watch where you step when you get out of the car, but this collection of colorful critters is made of cement.

Born and raised around cement, it just seemed natural that when Bill grew up he'd keep his fingers in it. Haun's Cement Art began when an elderly lady asked him to make a couple portable lawn ducks—the standard ornaments were too heavy for her to move—and within a week he had orders for thirty more. But these aren't your run-of-the-mill lawn ornaments; they're solid, poured cement, two-dimensional, painted pieces. Bill has since "improved" on the ducks by giving them rosy cheeks and shaded bodies.

That was his first effort; his inventory has grown to 2,500 items, and each year he adds more. Some have been discontinued and others are out of stock because Bill and his wife, Kolene, can't keep up with the demand. Especially popular is the buzzard, but the Hauns make every woodland animal, household pet, and everyday character you can think of (prices range from $2 to $150). Bill's inspirations come from pattern books, T-shirts, coloring books, and the occasional artist, as well as from customer requests. He and Kolene work seven days a week, mixing, pouring, and painting, but they enlist the painting help of about thirty-two freelancers, most of them local senior citizens.

Kolene says they use latex enamel that has a fifteen-year durability. "We guarantee our work, except against abuse," says Bill. And what constitutes abuse? "Well, one fellow ran a chipmunk through his snowblower. Another guy took revenge on his girlfriend's favorite penguin and shot it with his .22—that's abuse." But he boasts that only the penguin's paint was chipped.

Most of his sales are to tourists from all over the world, some of

Buzzards and pandas and ducks, oh my. Bill and Kolene have them all . . . plus 2,497 others.

whom have asked Bill how he makes his cement cut-outs. But rather than give out his trade secrets—mold making is a closely guarded process—he's begun franchising. For a flat fee the new owner gets everything he needs to set up shop, plus protected territory.

Although his business is hardly portable, Bill's thinking of packing up and moving. But like he says, "It won't be hard to find us, just look for the tree with the buzzards in it."

★ *Directions:*
1 mile north of Plains on Montana Highway 200.

For more information:
Haun's Cement Art, 406-826-3334.

did you know...

2   Absaroka is pronounced ab-SORK-ee, Rapelje rhymes with apple jay, Pondera is pon-der-ay, and Meagher is mahr (good to know if you don't want to be branded a tourist).

Fairview

If you think life in the country is simple, you've never been to Fairview. This little town of 800 has enough quirks and oddities to keep anyone from getting bored. For starters it's so far east in Montana that it spills over into North Dakota. One of Fairview's streets is right on the state line. Ray Trumpower, president of the Fairview Chamber of Commerce, demonstrates how he can drive down the center line of State Street, or Interstate Avenue, once the main street in Fairview (but it's no longer the main street; that has been moved over two blocks and now the main street is Ellery Street) with the driver in Montana and the passenger in North Dakota. At which point he turns to you, smiles, and says, "And you're in the Central time zone and I'm in Mountain time," but adds, "that depends on who you talk to"—a phrase that could be the town's motto. Some locals insist the time zone runs down the middle of Main Street while others say it's one mile east of town at the Yellowstone River.

Straddling the state line has its advantages. When Fairview wanted to hold a paddlefish tournament, officials had to set up headquarters across the street in North Dakota because it is a protected species in Montana. And once when the annual circus came to town with its lion and tiger act, it chose to leave the big cats in North Dakota rather than deal with Montana's laws about bringing them into the state. In the future the circus will set up on the other side of the street.

There are a few minor disadvantages to the state line/time zone dilemma: For example, there's only one post office and it's on the Montana side, so about 100 people who live on the North Dakota side of town get their mail in Montana. Also, although each side has its own grade school, high school kids on the North Dakota side either pay tuition to go to the Montana side or trek sixty miles round trip to the nearest one in North Dakota. And Ray says he has to be careful every time he uses his wife's car because she has the clock set for Central time since she works across the state line. Any appointment or event needs to be double-checked to

A monument to beat all monuments, this gargantuan veggie and its comrades are the pride of downtown Fairview.

see what time zone it refers to. And because of the cemetery's location, it's not certain if some people are buried in Montana or North Dakota.

Another hot topic of discussion (and confusion) is Fairview's two lift bridges, the Snowden, the Fairview, and the Nohly. Ray grins: "Two bridges, three names." The Snowden crosses the Missouri in Montana, the Fairview crosses the Yellowstone into North Dakota and goes through that state's only tunnel. "The Nohly could be either bridge," says Ray, "depending on who you talk to." Both of the bridges were designed to allow steamboats to pass underneath, but unlike a drawbridge, the entire span was lifted straight up using nothing more than a 1-horsepower motor (about the size of a washing machine's) and incredible counterweights. They are thought to be the only two bridges of their kind in the country.

The Fairview bridge (built in 1914) has a lift section that can be moved according to changes in the river's channel, and almost everyone agreed until recently that neither the Snowden nor the Fairview had ever been lifted except for testing. So, imagine the excitement when a photo surfaced that showed the Fairview in the up position, but now the argument is whether it was for boats or when it was tested. Of course, Ray says, no one really cares; the whole bridge issue is good for discussion and argument's sake.

Today only the Snowden is used for rail traffic, but initially both bridges accommodated trains and cars. At the Fairview bridge this was especially harrowing. Train or car—only one could cross at a time. So booths at each end of the bridge were manned during the daytime: an approaching car would notify the booth attendant, who in turn radioed the other side to make sure no other traffic was coming (especially important when car met train). This worked fine as long as it was daylight and there was someone in the booth, but adding to Fairview's colorful past is the story of one woman who made the crossing sans booth guard and had to abandon her car midbridge when she met a train coming from the other direction.

Plans to demolish the Fairview bridge came as a surprise to the townspeople, who found out about it when an engineer who was working on a new bridge nearby accidentally showed up at a community meeting. Folks had been talking about the bridge for years, but the idea of actually losing it goaded them into action. Now the talk centers on what to do with it should they take possession from Burlington Northern, who would love to get rid of its iron white elephant. One idea is to allow foot traffic across the bridge that would take trekkers through the tunnel to an area with picnic tables. The tunnel has enough of a curve to put you in complete darkness when you're in the middle, which brought up another idea of putting timed switches at either end so you could experience total darkness. This discussion could go on for some time.

But so much talk can work up a thirst. If you're sitting in the Waterhole #3 Bar and you've argued time zones and bridges to death, and you've still got room for a couple more beers, just bring up the topic of the town's mayor, who, according to the local newspaper, was arrested several times for DUI. One of his stunts got him mentioned on Paul Harvey's radio show. It seems the fine mayor was under the influence in Yellowstone National Park and decided to take two bear cubs back to Fairview. That's a federal offense, which got him arrested for unlawful possession and illegal transportation. His latest escapade of driving a motorcycle through the Waterhole and out the front door, then crashing into a wall was enough to cause the city to ask him to step down. He said no, and they said oh. They had no idea what to do next, and as it turned out there wasn't much they could do—it's beyond their authority since he's an elected official. And he still is, because he was reelected, but then again, Ray reminds us, no one ran against him.

So the beet goes on—sugar beets, millions of them. In fact, in the center of town is a monument dedicated to them . . . and wheat, and

The Fairview bridge has had its share of ups and downs, mostly downs, depending on who you talk to.

cows, and soon to come, bees. Fairview's claim to fame (the smiling sugar beet on its website says so) is that it's the sugar beet capital of Montana and North Dakota. Getting the title wasn't all that hard—they just asked. Ray says, "Although other parts of both states produce more beets, we're the only ones who approached the governors, and since no one else had ever asked, they said okay." Each business takes turns displaying the framed certificates signed by both governors. The anatomically correct beet is crafted of fiberglass and stands about five feet high; leaves add another two or three feet.

Despite all that Fairview has on the line, the people here are friendly, honest, and awfully proud of their berg; it's a community where everyone looks out for each other (it's a good thing, too, because if you call the police department after 5 P.M., weekends, or sometimes during lunch, you'll get an answering machine). And they all have a great sense of humor. Ray says, "You almost have to, to live here." Fairview has always been a laid-back place; in fact, the story goes that before there was a town, a bar sat on the bench overlooking the valley. From the back porch, a patron looked out and remarked, "Now that's a fair view." Nobody argued, it didn't depend on who you talked to, and the name stuck. Innocuous beginning, wonderful history. But folks here really do live on the edge—if only they could agree just where that is.

★ *Directions:*
Northeast Montana where Montana Highway 200 crosses the state line.

For more information:
Fairview Chamber of Commerce, 406-747-5259.

did you know...

3 The headwaters of the second largest river in the United States can be found in Three Forks, where the Gallatin, Jefferson, and Madison meet to form the Missouri.

Lone Grave, **Neihart**

On September 19, 1891, Alexander Campbell put down roots in the Little Belt Mountains—permanently, that is, for all eternity. At least that's what his gravesite reads. Unfortunately no one knows for sure who he was, where he came from, or what he died of. Locally known as the Lone Grave, his site lies about 3 miles south of Neihart and 100 yards to the east of the road at the forest's edge. His final resting place is about as peaceful as it gets: no superhighway, no subdivision, no shopping mall—just the occasional *rawk* of a raven or wind in the pines.

A dotted line on the Montana highway map shows U.S. Highway 89 as a scenic drive and Neihart as an early mining camp, but there is nothing to indicate Alexander Campbell's final resting place.

Up until just a few years ago, motorists gawking at the scenery along this stretch of National Forest Scenic Byway would have passed the grave without noticing it. But, through the efforts of the Federal Women's Program of the Lewis and Clark National Forest, Alexander's plot has been given a revamping. The women carefully repainted the date on his severely rotted marker, matching the original dark green they found there. They tore down the old decayed fence and erected an identical one, this one with screws rather than the nails that held for only 100 years.

But is it Alexander who is resting beneath the pines? Local rumors say it could be Alexandria Campbell, a fourteen-year-old girl who was accidentally killed while her father was grouse hunting. She supposedly was resting under the pines when the gun went off. The rumor is thought to have started because the last few letters of Alexander's marker were hard to read.

Historians have dispelled the idea that Alexander was related to Neihart pharmacist Thomas Campbell, who came to the area in 1894. They agree that he was most likely a sheepherder, but then speculation takes over. Did he die of natural causes? The plague or flu perhaps? Or was it, as some say, murder? There is no evidence of a homesite and no one knows how old he was when he died. The answers were buried with Alexander.

★ *Directions:*
U.S. Highway 89, about 70 miles south of Great Falls.

Duck-billed Giant Hadrosaur,
Ekalaka

Eastern Montana is prairie country. Stand in this part of Carter County and look around—what you'll see is grasslands, grass lands, grasslands, and Ekalaka. Lying on one of the county's two paved roads, it's a town not on your way to anywhere else, which is exactly how it started. The story goes that a buffalo hunter with plans to start a saloon was passing this way when he got stuck in a snowdrift. So he decided that anywhere in Montana was a good place to build a saloon, and Ekalaka was born. But it didn't get its name until it became a town. Ijkalaka, an Oglala Sioux, was the niece of Red Cloud and a distant relative of Sitting Bull. Raised by a white family, she became the wife of David Russell, who paid her father eight horses and a 100-pound sack of sugar.

All the usual Montana history is here—ranching, Indians, homesteaders, cowboys—but while riding cows, Walter Peck, an amateur geologist, made the discovery of the state, actually of the United States. In 1930 he found the complete remains of a duck-billed hadrosaur, one of only three in the world (although all were found in this region, the other two are in New York City's Museum of Natural History).

Peck knew he had found something important and wanted to share it with the rest of the world, so he and two other men founded the Carter County Museum to house their treasure. They bought an old garage and raised funds to add on to it. Under the auspices of the Carter County Geological Society it became the first county museum in Montana. Peck's dinosaur had a home.

Meanwhile, Marshall Lambert, a cousin of the Russells, left Ekalaka for college and the service, all the while his interest in paleontology increasing. He hoped to go back to his hometown and work with Peck, but shortly after his return Peck died. So by default the museum became

This hadrosaur was thirty feet long and eighteen feet tall on its hind legs, and thankfully, a vegetarian.

Marshall's, and he served as director for the next fifty years. He was more than an amateur geologist—he lived for paleontology—some might call him obsessed. Most locals agree he was brilliant but disorganized. Although not interested in displaying his finds, he did have a hand in creating the setting. He designed the museum's inner walls, not too note-worthy normally, but these are made of petrified wood, giving you the feeling of being back in time—inside a big tree. The rock is from within forty miles around Ekalaka.

Warren White and his wife, Shirley, took on the task of sorting out box after box of Marshall's accumulations. Spurs were pulled from among brachiopods and fossils separated from bullets. They came across a slab of slate embedded with an ichthyosaurus fossil that Marshall had finagled from Princeton University. The 100-million-year-old specimen was dusted off and given a place of honor. The results are some of the finest displays you'll find in any Montana county museum.

More than 75 million years ago, dinosaurs walked Ekalaka's main street. As part of the large inland sea that covered much of Montana and make it a paleontologist's paradise, the area is fossil rich. Found near town and on display in the museum are a mammoth tusk, a complete triceratops skull, a small tyrannosaur, and a dome head

(*Pachycephalosaurus wyomingenisi*)—all have been verified by the Smithsonian Institution.

Today 4,000 to 5,000 visitors annually come through the museum. Some want to see the Indian artifacts like the 1890s shell dress, others are interested in the collection of Western rifles and firearms, and some come to Ekalaka in spring and fall to herald the arrival and departure of the western meadowlark—locals celebrate it with festivals. But the real star is still the duck-billed hadrosaur.

The road to Ekalaka from Baker is thirty-five miles of stick-straight asphalt. In the winter the highway's gentle dips turn into windswept drifts. People are sometimes isolated for days before a plow comes through. Come to think of it, that's how the town got started.

★ *Directions:*
35 miles south of Baker on Montana Highway 7.

For more information:
Carter County Museum, 406-775-6886; call for hours.

Sheep Drive, **Reedpoint**

J ust off Interstate 90 a sign on an old building reads, "Welcome to Reedpoint, MT. Population 96. Sheep Drive Capital of the World." But today that population has swelled to nearly 10,000, not including sheep. This is Labor Day weekend, more popularly known as Sheep Drive weekend, when woolly critters transform this one-street town into an ocean of fleece.

Up until ten years ago this was known as Bachelor Day, which was nothing more than one big adult party. According to Chuck Egan, man in the know, the sheep drive was begun to honor the sheep industry just as the cattle drive of 1989 honored the beef growers. "Contrary to rumors, it was not because we felt we were snubbed during the '89 cattle drive," says Egan. The sheep drive's first year saw between 5,000 and 6,000 visitors, but "we've had as many as 25,000 people here. It's such a great community thing—locals and out-of-towners getting together and having a good time. Every town needs a sheep drive."

The original promoters, Russ and Connie Schlievert, present-day owners of the Hotel Montana, managed to garner national attention for the event, ranging from newspaper coverage in Australia to the front page of the *Wall Street Journal*. Today the popularity of the drive has their bed and breakfast booked for Sheep Drive weekends through 2002. A bonus of staying at their place includes a selection of period clothing available to lodgers interested in "dressing for the occasion."

The festivities begin around noon but people show up as early as 9:30 to watch sheep-related demonstrations and vendors setting up. Things really get moving shortly after noon with a parade featuring a sheep-oriented theme, of course, from live animals in the back of a pickup to a young parader with cotton balls stuck all over her body and rosy pink cheeks.

Sheep puns show up everywhere on hand-lettered as well as commercial signs: Reedpoint Welcomes Ewe. Just about any telephone pole has a

It's Labor Day weekend in Reedpoint, and they're baaaack. Main Street becomes wool-to-wool sheep.

flyer stapled on it listing the day's events, which feature a sheep-shearing demonstration, yarn spinning, log sawing, and teamster competitions, and culminates in the early evening with a dance. One of the most popular events, however, is the egg toss, which is held in the street in the center of town. Teams line up. For $1 you and a partner can buy an egg, which is tossed between you at increasing distances until the last team remains with an intact egg.

The main street is lined with vendors selling crafts, yard sale items, antiques, soft drinks and beer, and food. (The Montana Woolgrowers Association sells—in addition to lanolin-based hand cream and sheep notecards—BBQ lamb sandwiches.) Other booths run the gamut from buffalo burgers to woolen socks to face painting. And at more than one location $10 will get you an "official" Sheep Drive T-shirt.

The drive of 1998 hosted the largest flock of sheep ever, according to Jerry Friend, one of the many drive promoters. He explains that a flock equals about 40 to 50 sheep, whereas a band is 1,000 to 1,200—this particular year featured a band. Although the herd consists mostly of Targhee sheep, a few goats are mixed in as markers. (A sheepherder may have four marker goats, for example, that stand out in the crowd, allowing him to quickly determine by their presence that all is well with the

flock.) Predators are a real problem out here, Friend says, mainly coyotes, and in addition to guard dogs, the goats help to protect the flock.
The sheep make a round trip of twenty-eight miles from their home ranch
to town and back again; they're pastured overnight just outside town.
They make a dry run of the route the night before the big event, their
droppings marking the scent for the real thing the next day.

The entire day focuses on a run that lasts three to four minutes, but
during that time the streets are a sea of sweaters-to-be. The aftermath is
a minefield of Silly String, broken eggs, and sheep droppings, but no one
seems to care what gets stuck to their shoes. Even Senator Max Baucus
picked his way through the mess to greet constituents in 1996 (it was an
election year).

In 1998 sheep reigned and rained. A new feature that year caused
more than its share of publicity for the Sheep Drive and unforeseen head-
aches for the promoters, who told the media that 100 sheep were going
to be dropped out of airplanes. Word got back to animal rights activists
100 miles away in Bozeman, and the sheriff was sent to investigate. The
promoters—tongue-in-cheek—said yes it was true, but the animals would
be wearing parachutes (which indeed they were). Initially, no one both-
ered to mention that the sheep were about three inches high and stuffed
with polyester. Children retrieved sheep from lawns, bushes, and tree-
tops to exchange them for free soda pop. Next to the real thing, they
were the hit of the drive.

Teamsters in Reedpoint have nothing to do with the auto industry.
On the contrary, these folks deal with mules. In 1998 wagon trains from
Absaroka (ab-SORK-ee) and Rapleje (rhymes with apple jay) arrived to
participate in the teamsters competitions. George Miller, at eighty-seven,
is the oldest member and wagon master. Among the day's events held on
the north end of town is a teamster pull in which the mule tows behind it
a log roughly the size of a telephone pole and through the handler's skill
wends its way through pylons—the object being to not go out of bounds
or knock over a marker. Speed is definitely not a factor because the handler walks alongside carefully guiding the mule. Or you might thrill to
the mule that pulls a cultivator and its rider through soda-can corn rows—
knock over a can and lose a point. These events and others in town are
done as a Calcutta. The lucky winner of a Calcutta gets the bid on a team
and shares in the winnings.

There will never be a lack of festivals anywhere in Montana or throughout the United States for that matter, but the Sheep Drive, which ranges
from camp to cool, is one ewe don't want to miss.

★ *Directions:*
Interstate 90 in south-central Montana midway between Billings and Bozeman.

For more information:
406-326-2288.

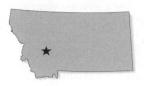

Free Enterprise Radon Mine,
Boulder

What's 400 feet long and cures damn near everything? According to thousands of patrons, it's the Free Enterprise Radon Mine in Boulder. Bobby and Brenda Shepherd from Georgia claim it relieved their gout. Jim Gatschet from Missouri says it took care of his arthritis. And Phyllis Newdorff from Texas swears it's the solution for her lupus.

What many homeowners are spending a fortune to get rid of, others are paying good money to inhale. Radon—the radioactive gas that comes from the breakdown of uranium—certainly has its detractors, as well as its fans. For years the EPA has been telling us how bad radon is in our homes. In Montana, "the radon capital of the United States," the state has determined that the exposure limit for mine visitors is 32 hours per year—one-tenth the amount uranium miners may experience before exceeding the safe range. Mine owners Pat Lewis and Burdette Anderson suggest three one-hour mine visits per day over a ten-day period. There is also a mandatory two- to four-hour break required between hourly visits.

Radon is colorless, odorless, and tasteless, so how do you know you're getting your money's worth? Just ask Burdette. With a geiger counter he shows you the radioactivity in a piece of uranium that he keeps on the counter for just such purposes. Then from his desk drawer he pulls out an old Fiesta Ware platter—the geiger counter ticks like crazy (he stresses that it's only the old orange glazing that's radioactive).

The mine was started in 1949 by Pat's grandfather, Wade, when uranium was discovered in the hills west of Boulder. Two years later a miner's wife reported remarkable relief of her bursitis after visiting her husband several times in the mine. By 1952 the radon mine had become a gold

Skeptics are welcome to take a free tour. Or you can pick up a brochure that lists testimonials—with phone numbers—from satisfied inhalers.

mine as thousands began to arrive in search of the magical healing powers down its eighty-five-foot shaft.

But mine attendance began to drop in the early 1990s when the EPA encouraged people to rid their homes of what it considered dangerous levels of radon. Recently, however, a heightened interest in natural healing and holistic medicine is bringing people back.

Although there are numerous radium hot springs found throughout the United States, Montana has the only underground radon health mines. From a peak of sixteen mines only six remain; all are located between Butte and Helena in the area surrounding Boulder. The Free Enterprise Mine was not only the first radon health mine, it was the best. And unlike its counterparts, it's the only vertical-shafted mine of the bunch.

Being the best has a price, of course. Ten days of elevator rides fetches $150; a one-hour dose will set you back $5. After paying the fee, you can board the elevator to the tunnel where you'll spend the next 60 minutes; it's not for anyone in a hurry—the elevator takes 90 seconds to get to the

Not much of a view, but after all, you're eighty-five feet underground. You can spend your entire hour reading names and addresses left by visitors on the wooden walls.

bottom. You may want to come armed with a blanket as the mine's temperature is a year-round 58 to 62 degrees, although heat lamps have been installed to ward off the chill.

To while away the hour, your hosts have provided tables with board games and stacks of magazines. If that doesn't keep you busy, consider adding your name to the hundreds on the tunnel's timbers, but please don't scribble on the rock walls.

Claustrophobic? There's the Inhalatorium, an upstairs room where radiated air is drawn up from the depths through ductwork. Have pets? Fluffy and Fido are welcome, but not underground. Kennels are provided free of charge for your animal friends to soak up the rays.

Clients run the gamut from General Omar Bradley and the Amish to nurses and bricklayers. The majority seem to be seniors or those afflicted with arthritis. Many are Canadians and Midwesterners—just take a look at the Where Are You From map on the lobby wall.

Not everyone who gets "shafted" sees results, however. About seventy-five percent claim some sort of improvement, ranging from noticeable to complete relief of their symptoms. We spoke to one regular from Oregon who visits the mine twice a year. She swears she couldn't lift her arm before she came here, then demonstrated a grand slam–caliber swing—a glowing recommendation.

While sitting among radioactive rocks eighty-five feet below the earth may not be your idea of a good time, lots of people around the world would disagree with you. The mine's owners make no claims as to its medical benefits and advise you to consult your physician before and after visits. Does it work? You be the judge. Reservations aren't needed—just drop in.

★ *Directions:*
Just off Interstate 15 halfway between Helena and Butte.

For more information:
406-225-3383; www.lewis@radonmine.com.

did you know...

4 The Roe River in Great Falls claims to be the world's shortest river at 200 feet, but so does the D River in Lincoln City, Oregon. Giant Springs, the source of the Roe, is the largest freshwater spring in the United States, no dispute there.

Ismay *(Joe)*

As you pull into Ismay, three words come to mind—witness protection program. If you find yourself here, either it's intentional or you're really lost. Nestled in a draw six miles from the nearest paved road, this was once a bustling town of 400. Now nearly a ghost town, with only about nineteen residents, it has endured more hardships than it deserves. Over the years passenger rail service, the town's lifeblood, was cut; a cyclone leveled the better part of the business district; and when U.S. Highway 12 was built it bypassed the town entirely. The final blow was dealt when the school closed in 1960, shutting down what few businesses were left—only the post office and Nemitz's Ismay Grain Company remain. McNamara's Store, Trail Café, Wilson Chevrolet Garage, Milwaukee Hotel, and about a dozen others are nothing more than historical markers in empty lots.

Even its name has suffered, going from one identity crisis to another. The town began in 1868 as Camp Custer, which it held on to for forty years. Then in 1908 when the post office opened, they named it Burt, but this stuck for only a month. That's when railroader George Peck came through southeastern Montana, naming railroad towns after his daughters: the result was Ismay, a combination of Isabell and Maybel, which lasted for eighty-five years. In 1993 a phone call brought yet another name change.

A Kansas City radio station decided a town would be the perfect gift for their beloved Chiefs quarterback, Joe Montana. Looking for a small town in Montana, they decided on Bearcreek, but were turned down. Number two on the station's list was Ismay. Needing funds to operate their volunteer fire department, the twenty-two Ismayans unanimously voted to change the town's name to Joe in hopes of selling caps, T-shirts, mugs, and so on that read, "Joe, Montana."

To kick things off in Ismay, er Joe, they dubbed their Fourth of July celebration Joe Montana Day and planted a Welcome to Joe, Montana

For the past seven years, Joe Montana may have driven past this sign on U.S. Highway 12, thinking it was pointing to Joe Mountain.

sign at the edge of town. They also created a toll-free number (no longer available) for merchandise, which led to interviews and international exposure, including one reporter from France. Their game plan paid off. They needed just a few thousand dollars to retrofit a fire truck, but according to the mayor's wife, Rita Nemitz, "we had enough to build a huge fire hall with a kitchen, bathrooms, and office plus a three-truck bay, as well as a community hall."

When negotiations were done Ismay had agreed to change its name (on an honorary basis) to Joe every year from the Fourth of July through the Super Bowl. On the plus side, the radio station agreed to fly the entire town to Kansas City as special guests at a Chiefs game, where they met Joe. Everyone came out a winner, even the Chiefs. "We won by two," says Rita. Part of the deal also called for Joe to show up in town, but he never did. They haven't given up hope, though; they still send him an invitation to Joe Montana Day every year. Maybe next year . . .

★ *Directions:*
Midway between Miles City and Baker off U.S. Highway 12.

For more information:
For a flyer of Joe, Montana, products, call 406-772-5743.

Ismay's post office sees to it that Joe Montana's invitation is sent out each year.

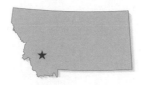

Humbug Spires Special Recreation Management Area

Not every excursion into the backcountry has to be a major event, but if you're looking for something more than a picnic in the park, consider Humbug Spires. South of Butte and just a few miles east of Interstate 15, the rolling countryside is punctuated by nine 300- to 600-foot-high granite monoliths that beckon hikers and rock climbers.

Faulting and erosion have left this cluster of needle-like spires, thus their name. Accounts vary as to the age of the rock outcropping—from 70 million to 2 billion years old—but the point is, they're really old. It's quite likely, however, that they are part of the Boulder batholith that's easily seen when you drive from Butte to Whitehall through Homestake Pass.

Exit at Moose Creek Road and travel the 3.5 miles to the parking lot where you'll find a trail map and primitive toilets. The usual hike is about two miles one way, but you can continue and make a full day of a nearly nine-mile loop. The first mile or so is level and easy walking along Moose Creek and its pines, firs, and aspens, then the trail climbs, sometimes over boulders, and you find yourself among Douglas-firs that are more than 200 years old. The farther you go, the harder it gets, so let your sense of adventure be your guide.

Walk quietly and you might see golden eagles, beavers, moose, mule deer, porcupines, or elk. Speaking of elk, it's wise to know Montana's hunting seasons; if you go to the Spires then, be sure to wear blaze orange, and don't forget your camera.

★ *Directions:*
Exit 99, Moose Creek Road, off Interstate 15, midway between Butte and Dillon.

For more information:
Bureau of Land Management, 406-494-5059.

did you know...

5 Beaverhead County is the third largest in size in the United States; Dillon, its largest town, has a population of 4,000.

Pathway Through *the* **Bible**, Joliet

In the beginning there were rocks. Twice a year Verdine White vacuums them. But these are not just any old rocks, they are of biblical proportions and they're in her backyard. They were there when she and husband, Rick, bought the place in 1982, and the next time you're passing through Joliet you're welcome to stop in and see them. Look for the sign that reads Pathway Through the Bible; it's next to the open gate and huge welcome sign.

The rock garden beyond the gate was the creation of German immigrant Adolph Land, who moved to Montana from Iowa in 1952 with his wife, Helen, and a small pile of rocks. They supported themselves by selling honey and then trees. Adolph decided to build a rock garden similar to the one he had in Iowa for the pleasure of his customers. But his background as a bible scholar and the encouragement of his patrons kept him busy building for the next twenty-three years. The result is Pathway Through the Bible, an elaborate display of biblical stories represented in rocks.

The rocks that Adolph had accumulated often inspired him as to which story he should depict. For example, petrified algae reminded him of Eve's hair, which led to his creation of Adam and Eve. Although Adolph would see something in the rocks, not everyone shared his visions. At times even he couldn't find an idea in the rocks until he built something—then he'd name it.

The Pathway, begun in 1957, includes more than twenty bible stories amid shrubs, flowers, and towering pines. Throughout the parklike setting, stone and rock combinations are artistically arranged, forming one acre of rockwork mosaic. Adolph started by building a tower to represent the Wise Men; he felt that because they were wise men they probably studied the stars, which is how they found the Star of Bethlehem. From the top of the tower you can see the rest of the Pathway as well as Granite Peak, Montana's highest point.

Visitors from as far as Germany and the Yukon Territory have walked under the rainbow of Mount Ararat. According to the guest register, many people have returned for a second or third visit.

As word spread of Adolph's project, people began to give him rocks, some from holy places like Vatican City and the Jordan River. These he worked into the floor of the Christ's Tomb structure, which he built with the same measurements as the Garden Tomb in the Holy Land. The half-ton rock at the tomb's entrance took four people with crowbars and ropes to move into place.

Look closely to appreciate Adolph's creativity. Attendees at the Sermon on the Mount, for instance, are represented by a sea of stone slabs set on end around the monolithic stone column symbolic of Christ. At the Crucifixion, however, observers are mere footprints in concrete tiles adorned with inlaid stones; Christ is a fallen stone crucifix. Stone-cast symbolism is everywhere, like the tilework mosaics of the spear and sponge at the Crucifixion scene and a cast sculpture of the rooster that crowed three times.

Equally impressive are Adolph's construction techniques—none more pronounced than the life-size stable, which took several years to finish. The domed ceiling was held in place with telephone poles until the cement hardened. A special touch in the stable is hay imported from Italy in the manger.

The Pathway is not without a woman's touch. In the floor of the stable is a mosaic Star of Bethlehem, one of Helen Land's contributions. She and an aunt did all of the mosaic work that adorns some floors, walls, and ceilings. A woman from Livingston added the carvings that appear on several of the flat rock items.

Rocks came from everywhere, the majority from Montana: sandstone from a blasting site nearby, travertine from Livingston, and petrified algae gathered in nearby mountains. Others, sent by friends, arrived regularly by train.

According to daughter Margo, "Sometimes when Mom and Dad went on rock hunting trips they took the back seat out of the car to make room for the rocks they'd bring back. Once the car was so full they couldn't pull out because it was scraping on the ground and the headlights were pointing up."

Not everything in the complex is set in stone, but it's no less interesting. The stairway to the tower is from the steamship *Josephine,* which once ran the Yellowstone; the pillars that form Solomon's porch are courtesy of a bank in Red Lodge; and a working lamppost boasts the mark of the Billings Foundry. But pay special attention to the praying hands at the Mount of Temptation: they're Helen's. Actually they were a gift to Helen that Adolph had coveted for the site. Helen said no, but upon returning from a trip one day found the hands firmly cemented in place.

Adolph was afraid of power tools, so everything was done by hand. Margo says, "Moving the rocks would have been comical had it not been so frustrating. No sooner had we created piles than Dad would want to build something there and we'd have to move them again." Thousands of used bricks were cemented in the walkways and structures—Helen cleaned every one by hand.

The last stone was cast in 1977, when Adolph was seventy-six. But that's not the end of the story. After Adolph died, Helen was looking for a buyer and Verdine and Rick wanted to move back to Joliet—a match made in heaven. The Whites weren't the only interested party, however, but when Helen asked the other buyer what his plans were, he said he was going to doze the whole thing under. The Whites' prayers were answered. Today the Whites maintain the property with the reverence Helen had hoped for. The local congregation assembles here each Easter for sunrise services, Verdine gives tours to youth groups, and more than one bride has walked down Adolph and Helen's pathway.

They've never advertised, yet the guestbooks overflow with entries from all over the world. Verdine says, "We're always open. Come park and help yourself." Even though maintenance is minimal, Verdine does make her semiannual trek to the garden with vacuum in hand. She claims it's to clean up the pine needles that have fallen into crevices, but it could be she just enjoys the peace and tranquillity that Adolph intended.

★ Directions:
18 miles south of Laurel on Montana Highway 212.

For more information:
There is no fee and no posted hours; it's always open. You are free to wander through the garden, but please respect the property owners' privacy.

Scene Along the Way

Orville Quick, **Circle**

"Come on in," he said, before I even knocked on the door.
"But you don't know who I am."
"That's okay, come on in; I'll find out later."

O rville Quick, an entertaining tinker who thoroughly enjoys his role as town eccentric, has a pretty good idea why strangers show up on his doorstep in Circle. Like us, most of them want to see Big Orville, the king of lawn ornaments—a three-ton, thirty-one-foot-long, twelve-foot-high cement brontosaurus.

The first question that comes to mind is, Why. And Orville will tell you, "Why not! It was a challenge. I'd done smaller sculptures," the putterer says, "but wanted to do something on a larger scale." Indeed, Big Orville (named by two little girls who came to see it) was not Circle's first Quick creation. A statue of George McCone (the senator for whom the county is named) and a three-foot-tall triceratops watch over the McCone County Museum. Also on site is his pièce de résistance—the lady and child he created for the state's 1989 centennial in recognition of the pioneer women of Montana. "I knew the county couldn't afford to buy a statue, so I offered to make one. They told me it couldn't be done, so of course I did it." It was a hit; when the statue was unveiled the lieutenant governor was there to dedicate it.

The energetic seventy-seven-year-old *artiste de cement* began his mammoth undertaking with a scale model (now affectionately known as Little Orville) before mixing up his first batch of cement. A local welder helped build the frame of rebar and chicken wire while Orville supervised. Construction began April 1, 1998, and thirteen bags of cement and four months later, *Brontosaurus quickii* was born.

Orville hoped to park his dino on a flat hilltop at the edge of town and had almost completed arrangements with the Air National Guard to

To keep the cement from falling through the wire frame mesh, Big Orville was stuffed with wadded newspaper. Grandson Bobby did the belly work.

have it helicoptored there, but the landowner backed out. Later the Glendive Chamber of Commerce showed interest, but Orville's $5,500 asking price wasn't in their budget, and that too fell through. So what to do with three tons of hardened cement? Wait until December and hang Christmas tree lights on it—900 to be exact. To save money, Orville hung them on one side only. He laughs, "But it was worth it, I won $5 from the Kiwanis Club." Until he finds a permanent home for Big O, he plans to move it to the back of his property but not until after harvesting the cucumbers planted under its stomach and tail.

The neighbors kept an eye on the goings-on but weren't too concerned—this wasn't Orville's first backyard project. Rock-and-cement storage sheds, myriad walkways, and terraced rock gardens reflect his creativity, as well as his penchant for cement. But most recently a huge mound of cow manure on a friend's ranch inspired Orville. He decided to market it as a potting soil, which led to another brainstorm, a machine to package the stuff in twenty-pound bags. Pieced together with a five-pound coffee can, plastic flower pot, and pieces of 2x4s, the contraption breaks up clumps and measures out the exact amount per bag. His first year he sold nearly 2 tons of MCM, or as his label reads, Plain Old

Montana Cow Manure—Packaged by Orville M. Quick, clearly reflecting his Quick wit.

The latest project on Orville's drawing board is a full-sized triceratops. But Circle winters are long, and that's when he does his best thinking, so it's anyone's guess what could show up in spring. But you can be sure it will have Orville written all over it.

★ *Directions:*
Circle is on Montana Highway 200.

For more information:
Ask anyone in town.

did you know...

6 *Flathead Lake has frozen over only seven times in the past fifty years.*

Carter, Virgelle, *and* McClelland **Ferries**

Y ou've traveled over miles of dusty, gravel road, through sage and grasslands, the only sign of life the occasional ground squirrel or pronghorn. The last bend in the road brings you to the banks of the Missouri River where you stop abruptly—there's no bridge. Fear not. Just honk your horn and almost like magic a benevolent being appears to whisk you across to the other side. It's a scene that's repeated daily April through October at Carter, Virgelle, and McClelland. These are Montana's ferry crossings and your highway tax dollars at work.

The free ferries are unique in that they are, first and foremost, free, but mainly that they each run on two cables, one for power and one to keep them from floating downstream—there are only six ferries like this in the United States.

Because each ferry averages only six crossings a day (mostly local ranchers or seasonal hunters), it's more practical for the state to pay operators an hourly minimum wage—out of which they are expected to buy their own gas to power the engines—than to build a bridge. Service is seasonal, however, and the ferries operate only during daylight hours depending on the Missouri's mood; water levels can't be too high or too low. You can cross at night if the operator's home, but it will cost. Donations for night service range from $2 to the box of chocolate-covered cherries that Grace Sanford at the McClelland ferry received from one grateful late-night traveler.

The savvy ferry-goer calls ahead not only to find out if the ferry is running but also to check on road conditions. All three sites are on gravel and dirt roads that can turn to gumbo, making them impassable when it rains. Even with the best-laid plans you may arrive at the river to find the ferry on the other side, but not to worry; it takes only a couple of minutes for it to come back—beep your horn and you'll be afloat in no time. Far from high tech, the ferries are powered by old tractor engines housed in a wooden shack set off to one side of the barge; cables running to towers on either shore span the river.

All operators are required to have a captain's license, but Grace goes one step further and dons her hat for special crossings. She and Susan run the ferry in shifts.

If the river is high enough you may share the ride with another vehicle, but by midsummer it's usually a solo trip. One large truck will max out the ferry's capacity. When the river's running normal it's about 600 feet across and 12 feet at its deepest.

If you cross the Missouri at Virgelle, Beverly Terry is likely to be your captain. A schoolteacher most of the year, she and her daughters run the ferry all summer. "Crossings are usually uneventful, although horses can be skittish, and that can be dangerous," she says. Her husband, Jimmy, pitches in when school's in session but spends most of his time just down the road at the Virgelle Mercantile. Once the center of this river crossing town, the Victorian mercantile now serves as an elegant bed and breakfast, but if you're looking for something different you can opt to sleep in their gussied-up sheep wagon.

Farther upriver is the Carter ferry where you'll find Brian Perkins at the helm, but the real captain is his Dalmation, Jack, who's made every crossing for the past two years.

Brian has piloted the craft for three years, "although I've been here for twenty off and on," he remarks. When he took over, he inherited a ferry that had sunk five times, once with a load of grain and once with cattle. "And back in 1952 an operator drowned"—a low point in the ferry's history.

Get out of your car, stretch your legs (not too far), and enjoy the ride. Too bad it lasts only a couple minutes. You may share the river with pelicans, cormorants, or an occasional great blue heron.

The McClelland ferry (or Stafford ferry, depending on which side you're coming from), in the Missouri breaks, has the most knock-your-socks-off rugged setting. But be forewarned, it's an incredibly steep 800-foot descent and climb back out—not for anyone pulling a trailer or driving an RV. You may want to double-check your brakes, too. At the bottom of this chasm sits a vintage mobile home that has served for the past six years as office and living quarters for Grace Sanford and her daughter Susan. Here the traffic can get heavy, especially during the fair in Lewistown. On this afternoon there were five cars lined up waiting to cross, but Grace says that the record is thirty-nine in one day. She's proud of their safety record: "We've never had a ferry break loose."

Wearing a long denim dress, Grace dons her white captain's cap, which does little to cover hair long enough she could sit on it. She's taking across some of her favorite passengers—kids. "I have a large bell just for them." As one child clangs the bell, the cables slacken and timbers creak, and another crossing is under way.

★ *Directions:*
Carter is 20 miles northeast of Great Falls off U.S. Highway 87; Virgelle is 30 miles northeast of Fort Benton off US 87; McClelland is 45 miles north of Lewistown.

For more information:
Virgelle, 406-378-3194; Carter, 406-734-5335; McClelland, 406-462-5513.

Montana Mule Days, **Drummond**

If you're looking for a good time the second weekend in June, get your ass to Drummond. "It's like a big family reunion," says Jane Lambert. She's referring, of course, to the annual Montana Mule Days, and she ought to know, she's been coming for years. The three-day event has been attended by jackasses from throughout the West for more than twenty years ("some even brought their mules," chuckles a veteran muler). In 1999, 180 mules—not including the donkeys and one zebra—showed up at the rodeo grounds.

"It really is a family affair," says the T-shirt lady Ellen Worth. She's been selling Mule Days–wear since 1985, with the profits going to the Montana Longears Association. "We're here strictly for fun, not cash prizes," Jane adds. "The prizes are real nice but nothing you'd run over your best friend for—we're not cutthroat." The association was formed to promote mules and donkeys, and its structure is as laid back as many of the mule owners. Jane remarks, "Our dues are only $10 a year and we have no officers or formal meetings, but we really look forward to seeing each other in Drummond once a year."

Understanding the genetics involved in breeding these animals is like refolding a road map. To keep it simple: donkey, ass, and burro—they're all the same animal. A mule is the hybrid of a male ass (jack) and a female horse; 99.9 percent of the time the mule is sterile. A hinny is the same as a mule genetically, but it's a cross between a male horse and a female ass (jennet). An average mule will fetch about $2,000, but "the sky's the limit," says one happy mule owner.

Beyond the grandstand is a sea of campers, tents, and horse trailers, and the public is invited to meet the animals and their owners. Rod and Lisa Thompson of the Rocking RL Ranch in Helena have nothing but praise for mules. Lisa says, "They're generally not as flighty as a horse, they're smarter, and they learn much faster. They also learn how not to do something much faster." Roper Lanier (he got the nickname from roping goats as a kid) of Idaho agrees and adds that you need more patience with a mule. He raises gaited mules, bred for their smooth riding. "If you get in a war of stubbornness, you've lost and you've got to start your training at square one." Lisa warns, "And when they kick they don't miss."

Friday kicks off the festivities with judging, log pulling, and jumping events. Although mules have traditionally been pack animals, on Saturday they become rodeo stars. Acting every bit the horse, they come alive for team penning, breakaway roping, and cow handling. But for good old family entertainment, Sunday's events can't be beat. Hundreds of spectators pack the grandstand, many with their dogs. The crowd is enthusiastic but civilized, breaking into cheers when judging the kid dressed as a carrot in the costume event. T. J. Silveira is the ten-year veteran announcer—the patriarch of this equine reunion. His Tim Allen voice and matching wit are frequently punctuated by a braying mule.

Crowd pleasers include the ride-a-buck, in which riders place a dollar bill under their knee while riding bareback at a walk, trot, then canter; as they lose their bills, they're eliminated. The flapjack race is a must-see. Armed only with pancake batter and three matches, riders must build a fire and cook an edible flapjack at least four inches in diameter while

If you think one mule can be stubborn, imagine the skill it takes to handle eight. This fellow not only has the right touch, he also knows what to say. His team follows every command.

keeping their untied animal within fifteen feet at all times. No event has a firm starting time except the first one each day at 7 A.M.—these folks work hard at having fun.

A dollar buys the show program, which describes more than 120 events and lists all contestants' names. From Axel to Zeke, the mules' monikers reflect their owners' creativity: Rocket, Bubba, Rant, Rave, Molasses, and Horse (wonder what *his* owner wanted for Christmas). Candy Allen owns, fittingly, the Candy Ass Ranch.

Those who can ride, do; those who can't are vendors. If it has to do with horses, mules, or donkeys it's here. Pick up a Donkey Belley hat or that set of chaps you just can't live without; better yet, get a new halter for your hinny. Of course many of the mules are for sale as well.

Although ass puns and jackass jokes abound, mule lovers take their animals seriously, but, says Jane, "We're here to have fun, and we do a good job of it." So bring the family but leave your image of stubborn mules behind—these asses are smart, just ask anyone who owns one.

★ *Directions:*
Just off Interstate 90 in Drummond, 55 miles southeast of Missoula.

For more information:
Montana Longears Association, 406-777-2331; longears@montana.com.

did you know...

7 Between Livingston and Bozeman on Interstate 90 is a ranch that lies in the median.

Wibaux **Ski** Festival

I t's the Fourth of July weekend, and there's snow on the ground, just
in time for the Wibaux Ski Festival, but no one's breathing a sigh of
relief. This snow isn't cold or wet—it's the down from cottonwood
trees. And the skis are not cross-country or downhill, they're Polish and
Nordic—Jablonski and Bjornski, for example. The festival is a tribute to
the area's large Polish and Norwegian population, many with names that
end in "ski."

For more than five years, the three-day celebration has begun with a
Friday night variety show. Then on Saturday, a midday parade is followed by a Polish barbecue held on the lawn at the Pierre Wibaux
Museum. Beneath the towering cottonwoods, 400 to 500 people munch
on baked beans, potato salad, and, to make it "ethnic," Polish hot dogs.
Missing are pirogies, potato pancakes, halushki, Swedish meatballs,
lingonberries—the killer stuff—but organizers are working on it for
future festivals.

In the afternoon, kids' games include a wild turtle race, in which turtles
are borrowed from nearby creeks and ponds to race their hearts out before they're returned home. There is also the greased pole climb, the op-
erative word being "pole." Then it's the big kids' turn with a ranch rodeo. Not your typical whoop-it-up, bronc-riding, testosterone-loaded
exhibition, this focuses on everyday ranch chores (and a few that aren't)
such as:

★ **cattle penning**: a half-dozen cattle are separated from a group and
herded into a pen.
★ **wild cow milking**: loose dairy cows are chased down; you must get
enough milk in a bottle to pour out.
★ **hide ride**: a horse is ridden at breakneck speed around the arena while
pulling a girl on a cowhide.
★ **horse saddling**: a six-person team in a pickup truck pulls into the
arena towing a horse trailer with two horses in it; while being timed,

The Dolajak band plays polka weddings, polka anniversaries, and even has a polka funeral on its résumé.

the horses are saddled, raced around the arena, then unsaddled and returned to the trailer. The event is not over until the truck's headlights are turned on.

For those who still have energy left, the evening ends with a street dance.

What Ski fest would be complete without a Sunday morning polka mass? St. Peter's Church is standing room only to hear Bob Dolajak and his daughter Julie Ternes, who have been imported from North Dakota for the special event. You haven't lived until you've tapped your feet to the "Battle Hymn of the Republic" or "What a Friend We Have in Jesus," polka style. Julie, who has written some of the hymns, sings and plays the electric guitar while accompanied by her father on the accordion. She encourages the congregation to sing along, and most do. Throughout the service, toes tap and heads bob in time to the oomp-pah-pah beat—even the liturgical responses are sung to a polka beat.

A mass like this can work up an appetite, and it just so happens that breakfast is served in the church basement. Then it's time to get down to business. The rest of the day consists of a massive horseshoe tournament, and horseshoes are taken seriously here—each hopeful entrant shoots fifty shoes to qualify.

You would almost expect closing ceremonies to cap off this long-weekend festival, but there are none—the crowd breaks up into smaller groups, which then slowly disperse until the only thing left is the camaraderie.

You don't have to be Polish or Norwegian to join the party; you don't even have to be a Montanan. But you can be sure that whether your name is Smith, Jones, or Sobiejeski, everyone here will make you feel welcome.

★ *Directions:*
Wibaux exit off Interstate 94 in eastern Montana.

For more information:
Wibaux Chamber of Commerce, 406-796-2412.

Bowdoin National Wildlife Refuge,
Malta

owdoin National Wildlife Refuge is a birder's paradise (note the
preferred term is birder not bird watcher; the birding community
has gone to great lengths to dispel the image of little old matrons
with high-top stockings knotted at the knees and binoculars hanging
around their necks). Birding has become America's number one specta-
tor sport, and millions of birders know it. Which brings us back to
Bowdoin, one of Montana's best places to see avian instinct in action.
According to refuge biologist Fritz Prellwitz, many of the visitors to the
refuge are not birders; they drop in just to see what all the fuss is about,
and there's plenty, especially in spring and fall when birds are courting or
migrating.

Not an area of mountains or even large hills, the refuge consists of
shortgrass prairie, wetlands, and fields that are attractive to waterfowl.
During migration, upwards of 40,000 geese and ducks create a constant
racket that becomes louder when they take flight. The area gets only
about a foot of rain annually, but the refuge is fed by the Milk River and,
in flood years, Beaver Creek, making this a major stopover and nesting
ground for thousands of birds.

Bowdoin's bird highlights appeal to birders and casual observers alike.
First are the sharp-tailed grouse, which put on an amazing display during
courtship in April and May. The process goes something like this: The
males go to the same lek, the dancing ground, early each morning to strut
their stuff for the females and defend their territories against other males.
Often two males will stare each other down, then with wings outstretched
they inflate air sacs in their necks and emit a cooing sound almost like
that of a mourning dove. It doesn't seem too threatening so far, but
then things get serious and they rapidly stomp their feet up and down
while dancing in a circle; now the noise they make sounds more like a

rattlesnake with a lisp. (If you're lucky enough to bump into Fritz, he'll give you a great demonstration of the actual rattle.) The dancing can go on for hours, but by midmorning the birds seem to disappear into the prairie until the next morning, when it begins all over again. It's about 2.5 fairly level miles to the lek, and the rewards are worth the effort.

Most people think of pelicans as coastal birds, and in the southern United States in winter, this is true of the brown and the white pelicans, but in summer the white species breeds inland throughout the western half of the country. No one at Bowdoin is surprised to see 1,500 pairs or more nesting here, but you may notice an almost eerie silence among the colony of so many birds, unlike the neighboring gulls who never seem to stop squawking. Lacking sharp talons or piercing beaks, they nest in colonies to protect the young and eggs from predators, but they are poor nest builders, laying two eggs in a depression on the ground lined with a few sticks. If you see a pelican up close you may notice an odd protrusion on the top of its bill—it's there, believe it or not, to attract females and usually falls off later in the summer. Although ungainly and clumsy on the ground, these huge birds are grace on the wing as they soar on air currents 100 feet above land or skim the water, their wings just kissing the surface.

Another species most birders hope to see court is the western or Clark's grebes. The national bird brains (aka the American Ornithologists' Union) have split this grebe into two species, but the difference is so minor it's hardly worth discussing—enjoy them as they are. These black-and-white ducklike birds have long, thin necks and pointy bills. The male and female participate in the courting ritual: They often face each other and bob their heads up and down, then side to side. When the time is right they both run across the surface of the water, side by side. They may go for twenty to thirty yards before settling down into the water to bob heads again.

Although not a refuge specialty (they can be found almost everywhere), the ever-present Canada goose looks gentle enough, but threaten its young and you could wind up with a serious bruise or broken limb. They fiercely defend their young, and with the leading edge of very strong wings have been known to break a dog's leg. As with all wildlife, it's best to admire them from a safe distance.

A not-as-visible but highly sought species by birders is the American bittern. More often heard than seen, this bird's distinctive *oonka-choonk* call gets a birder's adrenaline flowing. The bittern stands about 2 feet tall but when danger threatens, it stretches its neck and points the bill

While it may not look like much to us, to a female grouse it's Antonio Banderas and Brad Pitt rolled into one. Photo courtesy of Bowdoin National Wildlife Refuge.

skyward, making it appear almost another foot taller. But more important than height is its camouflage—the now exposed patterns on its neck blend in with the surrounding vegetation. We were fortunate to see this pose firsthand; what we weren't prepared for was that the bird came up the bank, walked to the middle of the tour road just a few feet in front of us, noticed our car stopped there, and immediately went into camouflage mode, with nothing to blend into but big sky. After a minute or so, it seemed satisfied that we were no threat, and finished its journey across the road. We thanked the bird gods and went on our way.

Catering to birders, hunters, and casual sightseers, prairie refuges like Bowdoin are crucial stopping points and breeding grounds for many species. They're not a bad stop for people either.

★ *Directions:*
U.S. Highway 2, 1 mile east of Malta; follow refuge signs.

For more information:
Bowdoin National Wildlife Refuge, 406-654-2863.

Scene Along the Way

Smith Mine Disaster, **Washoe**

ourists and locals alike travel Highway 308 every day on their
way to Red Lodge. As they come in from the east they marvel at
the mountains in the distance, and perhaps anticipate driving the
Beartooth—regarded by many as the country's most beautiful highway.
But little do they know that the small cemetery on the hill just outside
Bearcreek holds a big piece of Montana's history.

A short dirt road up the slope takes you to the cemetery, which is not
much more than a clearing in the fragrant sage. The scarlet Indian paint-
brush is a sharp contrast to the multicolored plastic flowers that adorn
some of the graves. A few plots consist of little more than a plain wooden
cross or a hand-painted marker. Some are in disrepair whereas others are
obviously tended to; several have photos of the deceased encased in glass
and set in the headstone; and still others, inscribed in Cyrillic, hint at the
area's ethnic diversity. This restful setting belies the catastrophe responsible for many of its occupants: Jules Besinque, died February 27, 1943;
Peter Giovetti, died February 27, 1943; John Hodnik, died February 27,
1943; James McNeish, died February 27, 1943; Frank Sumicek, died
February 27, 1943 . . . thirty-nine such markers in all.

February 27, 1943, was payday at the Smith Mine Number 3 in nearby
Washoe. Here were the best coal miners in the state. Ranging in age from
nineteen to seventy-two, they had settled in Montana, coming from all
parts of Europe—Ireland, England, Italy, Austria, Slovakia, and the
Balkans to name a few. Like every other day, 77 men entered the 8,000-
foot shaft, but on this day only three returned.

Deep in the mine there was an explosion, a blast so powerful it ripped
the clothing off men's bodies and embedded coal dust deep in their skin.
Men were knocked off their feet and swept along the floor. Those who
survived the blast succumbed to the resulting methane gas, which over-
took them quickly but painlessly. In their final moments a lucky few had
barely enough time to scribble their good-byes to loved ones on pieces of
powder boxes.

Ignance Marinchek was one of four men near the entrance when the explosion occurred. By the time he reached the door he was too weak to open it. Overcome by gas he died later in the hospital. The other three men survived.

Miners came from Red Lodge and Bearcreek to work in Smith Mine Number 3, which lies midway between the two towns. As a result just over half of the victims of the 1943 disaster are buried in Bearcreek; the rest lie in Red Lodge.

Rescue attempts were immediate. Men came from all over the valley to help, then later from Butte, Roundup, and even Salt Lake City. Some of the first rescuers tried to go in the mine before the proper equipment arrived but had to abort when they were overcome by the lethal gas (one died later in the hospital). It took eight days to get everyone out, six days just to reach the first ones.

Grief was indescribable. Dreams died with the men—one in particular was happy that this would be his last day in the mine because he and his family were moving to the farm he had worked and saved for. The disaster left in its wake fifty-nine widows and fifty-two fatherless children; one woman alone lost eleven relatives. It was also the beginning of the end for Bearcreek. Once home to about 3,000 people, today there are about 50 residents left in this scar of a town.

But the big question remains: What caused the explosion? Numerous investigations followed, each with a different conclusion. A commission appointed by the governor claimed "an accidental igniting of accumulated methane gas." The Montana state coal mine inspector said a cutting machine may have hit a pocket of gas, which was ignited by an open flame headlamp. The Federal Bureau of Mines, placing the explosion in a different area of the mine, also claimed an open flame lamp set it off. And Montana Coal and Iron Company, owners of the mine, placed blame on changes that federal inspectors forced on the mine, such as sealing off an area that created a buildup of methane.

Three months before the accident an inspector recommended eliminating open flame headlamps, but the country was in the middle of World War II and it would take months to comply because materials were in short supply. Concerned about the methane and headlamp issues, Montana Coal and Iron wanted to shut down the mine, but federal inspectors refused, citing the unusual demand of coal for the war effort. Ironically the miners were helping to win the war that indirectly killed them.

Remnants of the mine still stand along Highway 308 where an interpretive sign provides a brief history of the Smith Mine Disaster, but to get a true sense of what happened here on February 27, 1943, visit the Bearcreek Cemetery.

★ *Directions:*
The mine is 3 miles east of Red Lodge on Highway 308; the cemetery is 5 miles farther.

For more information:
The Carbon County Historical Museum in Red Lodge has detailed accounts of the mine disaster; phone 406-446-3667.

did you know...

8 *The lowest temperature was 70 below zero on Rogers Pass on January 20, 1954—it was a national record (source: a placemat in a café in Cascade, Montana).*

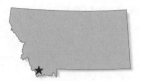

Yesterday's Calf-A, **Dell**

The sign for the exit on Interstate 15 says Dell, and you think surely you made a wrong turn because there's nothing here but a shed full of junk and an old brick building. But look again and you'll find one of the gems of the Treasure State—the Calf-A and Yesterday's museum.

Although never a hub of activity, Dell was an important stopover for travelers going between Bannack, the territorial capital, and surrounding ranches, assorted mines, and outposts. At one time it was a thriving little town, home to a hardware store, mercantile, railroad depot, hotel, stockyard, and schoolhouse.

The brick school building in the heart of "downtown" Dell was built in 1903 to educate the twenty or so students who showed up every morning for class. At the time there were seven or eight schools in a radius of thirty miles—about one school every ten miles—to accommodate the spread-out ranching population. It also wasn't a bad idea for schools to be easily accessible in the winter because traveling to school could be dangerous then in southwestern Montana.

The school in Dell stopped operating in 1963 when it was consolidated with the Lima school. Nine years later Ken Berthelson, seeking to purchase the bell in the old school's tower, dickered a deal that got him the bell as well as the school it was attached to.

The restaurant, which once housed students, now serves upwards of 30,000 diners per year. They come from all over the world. The guestbook has comments from Moose Jaw, Saskatchewan; Germany; the Netherlands; and one happy patron from New Jersey who wrote, "Roast beef like my mom makes." Seating is family style with six tables and six seats per table. You might end up sharing a table with the fellow from New Jersey or have the place to yourself depending on the hour or time of year.

Even though there are high ceilings and bare pine floors, there's a feeling of warmth here. Walls and shelves are crammed with school-day

Heavy metal takes on a new meaning in the sculpture garden where Ken's creations are part whimsy, part folk art.

Rising from the graveyard of buckboards, logging equipment, and mining machinery, the museum's facade is a display in itself, where wagon wheels, antlers, and saddles frame "Yesterday's," spelled out in horseshoes.

memorabilia. Pictures of George Washington and Abe Lincoln frame a faded flag on one wall.

The blackboard that once held reading, writing, and arithmetic, now has the menu written on it—from PBJ sandwiches to rainbow trout dinner (oddly the trout is a regular item whereas chili is seasonal). If you can't see the blackboard from your seat the waitress will provide you with a menu that stresses "real" mashed potatoes. The fries are fresh cut, too, and the patties are fresh burger—hand made, not prepattied or frozen. If you ordered salad with your meal, go to the head of the class because it's on the teacher's desk. Of course you can have too much of a good thing. The complimentary homemade jam that was once served in bowls was downsized to cups when patrons began eating it right off the table by the spoonful.

The restaurant is still a family affair, with Ken's granddaughter in charge, who says, "We've never advertised, we've never had to. But an interview on ABC's *20/20* sure didn't hurt." On this visit we were joined by one of Ken's senior relatives—a Calf-A regular—who was alternately eating, smoking unfiltered Pall Malls (don't look for a nonsmoking section), and getting up to bus tables or refill coffee for other customers. But she couldn't linger—she had to hurry home to split more firewood.

The inside of Yesterday's is even more cluttered than the outside but holds tons of memories. The only thing missing is . . . well, actually it's all here except Ken's gramophone.

The bell that first attracted Ken to the building still hangs in the café's tower. Surrounded by Dell's past, the old schoolhouse now serves breakfast, lunch, and dinner.

An example of Ken's handiwork, a "sawfish," hangs above the exit, hinting at what awaits in the outdoor sculpture corral. Here you'll see wildlife you won't find anywhere else in Montana. A bedpan-and-insulator bighorn sheep and a transmission-and-manifold moose gaze longingly at the shade of the steel rod, branding iron, and wrench tree while other indiscernible critters graze in the bare dirt pen. It's obvious Ken had a good sense of humor.

What Ken didn't weld together wound up in the museum next door. Here you're all too aware that dickering wasn't Grandpa Ken's primary trait—he was a pack rat, big time. Go around the back to the entrance of the museum and step inside to a veritable minefield of artifacts—thousands of them. Not your typical small-town museum, this is Ken's collection of what the people of Dell left behind when mining and logging dried up.

Highlights include a metal cooking center that held flour and spices touted to be "rat proof and fly tite" and an 1893 Montgomery Ward clothes washer (cost $3.45, new), but little else is labeled except for the "shinbone of horse" (just in case you had doubts) and a noose tagged, "vigilante snare."

If you're eyeing up the wooden wheelchair in the corner or the table that folds out into a bed, take care because Grandpa Ken's high-tech security system is watching you. This consists of a variety of handwritten signs such as: "Dont handle or see if they will work." "Dont steal. God will shurely see you and I might."

Not that his warnings aren't justified: His pride and joy—a gramophone—was stolen several years ago. Inside the foyer of the Calf-A hangs a sign that reads, "$250 reward for enuf information on the party who stole the old phonograph so I can shoot the sonofabitch—Ken." (After seeing the museum you'll wonder how long it took him to notice it was missing.)

Although Ken is no longer living, the town is still hanging in there, primarily because of him. You may not think of Dell as a destination hotspot but after exploring the museum, feasting on a home-cooked meal, and gaping at the sculpture whatnots, you *will* think of Dell.

★ *Directions:*
In southwestern Montana off Interstate 15.

For more information:
Yesterday's Calf-A is open seven days a week from 7 A.M. to 8 P.M.; 406-276-3308.

Big Sky's Lil' Norway Reindeer Farm, **Plentywood**

When you think of hobbies, stamp collecting and attending Star Trek conventions often come to mind; you'd have to go way down to the bottom of the list until you came across raising reindeer. But that's exactly what Gordon and Karla Aus do in their spare time. Karla decided they needed something different to occupy their recently purchased land, but what could they do on five acres? Somehow reindeer seemed to be the answer.

Karla's father read about the deer, and they researched it for a year until the time came to buy the three that Karla tracked down in Minnesota, but reindeer aren't cheap. So she needed a loan, and even though Gordon works as a loan officer he isn't allowed to lend to relatives; besides he was certain no lenders in their right mind would cough up $9,000 for three reindeer. "But, by darn she came home with the check," he laughs.

Deciding you want to raise reindeer is the easy part; going through the red tape of getting them is something else—after all, you don't just drop in at the humane society and pick up an abandoned reindeer. In Montana they're considered an elk, and you not only need a permit to own one, you're required to pen them with an eight-foot fence, and they must be certified tuberculosis and brucellosis free. The Auses turned to the University of Alaska for information on reindeer care and feeding, which gave them the confidence to expand their family with additions from Texas, Alaska, and Nebraska until it reached thirty head.

It's surprising just how small reindeer are: they stand about three feet tall at the shoulders with racks that practically equal them in size and weigh nearly twenty pounds. They're gentle animals (except for the males during rutting season), and wouldn't hurt a fly even though they absolutely hate flies. Eastern Montana summer heat doesn't faze them, but let a fly land on their legs or rump, for example, and they flinch,

Big Sky's Lil' Norway Reindeer Farm is a low-profile operation, and even at Montana's speed limit you might zip past without noticing their sign. Then again, you may not even see the deer—they prefer to hang out in a shed where they think the flies can't find them.

doing everything possible to get away from their tormentor. In fact, even though they have several acres to roam, they usually huddle inside a small shed—they think the flies can't get them there (we didn't say they were bright). So unless it's not fly season, you're not likely to see them from the road. Up close you can't help but notice their feet, which look like they're way overdue for a pedicure. But Gordon tells us that the splayed hooves are an adaptation to their native environment and help them walk on snow. Even so, they appear to be clomping around the barnyard wearing scuba flippers. Not as obvious as their feet are their noses—they're fuzzy, not smooth—built-in nose warmers that are more like a horse's muzzle than an elk or deer snout.

Eager to share these novel creatures with the world (and to have them earn their room and board), it wasn't long before the Auses bought a sleigh and started doing Christmas shows. One of their first gigs was at the mall in Missoula; it drew a larger than normal crowd, and Gordon and Karla weren't sure how their animals would react to so many people. As it turned out they were more nervous than the reindeer, who acted like pros and seemed to thrive on the attention. For indoor shows or in warmer climates their sleigh is equipped with wheels, which came in handy in Las Vegas. But it's not all glitz and glitter—"We almost froze at a show in North Dakota. It was minus thirty," says Karla. Some things are closer to home, such as the fundraiser in Plentywood where kids could get their photos taken with the deer. However, the bigger shows are expensive to do, and that Christmas spirit will cost the Auses $600 to $1,500 for a 6- to 8-hour day.

Besides doing shows, Gordon and Karla raise and sell the calves, which are just as gentle and curious as their parents. Even Dusty the dog has helped out: a newborn calf was rejected by its mother, and Dusty had a litter of pups, so a relative suggested putting the two together, and it wasn't long before the calf was nursing happily. Antlers, shed each year by the males and females, are in demand by craftsmen, providing yet another source of income. And just for fun, the Auses lug several of their stock to the annual Northern International Livestock Exhibition in Billings—just the place for Karla to scout out her next line of exotic livestock.

Although Plentywood isn't the North Pole, there are times when it sure seems like it. On a crisp December morning just going to the barn to feed the deer can put the Auses in a holiday spirit. Mingo, Dandy, Beau's Babe, and Flop Ears may not have the same ring as Rudolph, Donner, and Blitzen, but they can guide a sleigh with the best of them.

★ *Directions:*
3 miles west of Plentywood.

For more information:
406-895-2489.

did you know...

9 Wind in Livingston once blew over a railroad car; wind in Choteau is even worse, but according to locals there aren't as many people there to talk about it.

Mai Wah Society *and* Pekin Noodle Parlor, **Butte**

More than any other town in Montana, Butte has its landmarks. Coming from any direction you'd have to have your car windows painted black to not notice the Berkeley Pit. You also can't miss the headframes poised in Walkerville that overlook downtown Butte, or Montana Tech's large white M on the hill. And then there's the statue that gazes down on the pit. In town you'll pass by the Copper King Mansion, Arts Chateau, and the infamous Dumas Brothel. But tucked away on Mercury Street are two buildings that you probably won't notice; in fact, many of the locals aren't aware of them even though they are a large part of Butte's history. They are the Mai Wah and Wah Chong Tai buildings, all that remain of what was once Chinatown.

At one time Butte and the surrounding countryside had the largest Chinese population in the state, some say between 1,500 and 2,000, most drawn here because of the California Gold Rush. In the 1870s gold fizzled out in California and these Asian sojourners were forced to move on. Since things were not going well back in China—famine, revolution, crime, and a corrupt government—they headed north. Most who settled in Butte were entrepreneurs who provided goods and services and took on menial jobs. Others made their living off mining, but not underground; they took over abandoned placer mines. Whereas the Americans were looking to hit it big quickly, the Asians worked the placers hard and methodically, looking for a long-term return. And it paid off, but when the Americans saw how well the mines were producing, they reclaimed them, often violently.

Discrimination against the Chinese was widespread. State and federal laws penalized them simply for being Asian. But on a local level, the mining unions were some of the worst offenders. They boycotted Chinese-run businesses and any business that employed an Asian, fined union members who patronized them, and even threatened to fire employ-

The Mai Wah is the end of the line for the Chinese New Year parade. Even the dragon stops in for a cup of hot cocoa. When restoration is complete, the buildings will house another 400 to 500 artifacts.

ees just for living in a boardinghouse that used Chinese labor. Ostracized and harassed, the Chinese took strength and safety in numbers. But even Chinatown was no haven when the union began to station thugs in doorways of Chinese businesses to discourage customers from entering. One Chinatown resident spared this hostility was Dr. Huie Pock, a surgeon and physician who was well respected in the Chinese and American communities. And it was Dr. Pock who was instrumental in initiating a lawsuit against the unions to recoup money lost because of the harassment. He and his group "won"; they sued for $50,000, were awarded $1,750, and never received a penny, but the unions backed off.

Chinatown was a five-block area whose main street was a passageway called China Alley, adjacent to which are the Mai Wah and Wah Chong Tai. In addition to dealing in dry goods the Wah Chong Tai provided medical assistance, interpreters, postal services, an herbal store, and more; on the second floor was a restaurant. Next door the Mai Wah's second floor housed a noodle parlor with attached kitchen, its concrete floor showing wear from years of noodle making. But between the noodle parlor and the first floor is an unusual feature—a cheater story—another floor used mainly for lodging as it had only six-foot-high ceilings.

By the 1940s, a variety of factors including the decline of mining and World War II added to Butte's depression, and Chinatown became a virtual ghost town. All that's left is on display in the Mai Wah Society Museum. Although the buildings themselves are the main artifacts, there's plenty inside to keep Mary Kay McGrath—tour guide, society president, and general fixer upper—occupied. She'll gladly show you the antique paper kites and tell you that it's bad luck to pick one up off the ground (traditionally they are flown to carry away bad spirits). She'll also point out the hands-on tangram, seven geometric wooden shapes you can arrange in unlimited patterns. It's not likely that Mary Kay will forget to tell you about the Chinese lottery, also known as the white pigeon game. When the Butte chief of police shut down the lottery, the Lyden brothers modified it and took it to Reno, Nevada, in 1935, where it became known as keno. Mary Kay loves to talk about the antique mahjong game, opium pipe bowls, and articles from the dry goods store. Just looking at the 5-foot noodle rolling pin and huge bamboo steamer, you can almost smell the noodle parlor; in fact, you can—it's just around the corner, but it doesn't open until 5 P.M.

The Pekin Noodle Parlor is owned by Danny Wong, one of Chinatown's few remaining descendants. Climb the 26 stairs to the restaurant where you can feast on salmon—salmon wainscoted walls, salmon wainscoted booths, salmon booth curtains. But the decor doesn't stop there . . . well, actually it does. Except for the Victorian ice cream chairs and Formica tabletops, your dining booth is as sterile as a doctor's office. Yet overall, there's a sense of authenticity and a feeling that this is just the way noodle parlors always were.

For a genuine Chinese celebration, mark your calendar for late January to early February for Chinese New Year. You can even join in the parade—more than 300 do each year. The Mai Wah Society, organizer of the event, is proud of its new authentic dragon and rightfully so since their old one had a strong resemblance to Disney's Pluto. Dubbed the shortest, loudest, and coldest parade, it's a good time in any language.

★ Directions:
Mai Wah and Wah Chong Tai, 17 West Mercury Street, between Montana and Main Streets; Pekin Noodle Parlor, 117 South Main Street.

For more information:
Mai Wah Society, 406-723-6731; Pekin Noodle Parlor, 406-782-2217.

Little Cowboy Bar, **Fromberg**

Shirley Smith knows cowboys—she's not too bad at tending bar either. Although Fromberg is an easy spit on the map to miss, once in town it's pretty hard to ignore Shirley's Little Cowboy Bar. Obviously not part of a chain, it's done up in paint sale aqua and adorned with nearly 100 ranch brands of Shirley's family and friends. The wooden entryway has seen its share of spurs and boot heels, and sneakers seem somehow irreverent here. The metalwork star that hangs above the wooden "Cowboy Bar" sign is decorated with multicolored Christmas lights, but it's the sign underneath all this that tells you this is not an ordinary bar. It reads "Museum." Even before you go inside you know this place has character.

Shirley never intended to own a bar but she's had this one for twenty-seven years. Back in 1972 she was helping the owner get it ready for business, but "he beat the hell out of the state liquor inspector, so he didn't get his license." Rather than let her hard work go to waste, she jumped at the chance to buy the bar. She recalls that her first tip, still taped to the back bar mirror, was $1 from the notorious Della Mae, an African-American madam from Billings. Della Mae was well known regionally not only for her services but also because every Christmas she gathered up the city's derelicts and took them out for dinner.

Every bar needs a theme, and here's where the cowboys come in. Shirley was married to one—a working cowboy, she stresses, who died in true cowboy fashion, on the range with his boots on. Her husband was working for the Greenough Ranch at the time; thus began her connection with this world famous rodeo family. The Greenoughs are featured in the bar's decor up front, but grab your beer and head back to the museum for their full story.

The Greenough dynasty began in the 1880s the day Ben Greenough left New York City. This former paperboy was only sixteen when he headed west where he knocked around doing odd jobs, picking up the

One piece of Shirley's life nearly lost among the rodeo keepsakes is a photo of the ten-by-twelve-foot tool shed she was raised in. She lived here for nine years with her parents and four siblings.

name Pack Saddle Ben. For a while he and Calamity Jane cut and sold firewood near Red Lodge, but she turned out to be a bad business partner, so he drifted on. He began his rodeo career by winning the first bucking horse contest in Montana in 1898. Every year he rodeoed from Boston to Mexico, making a name for himself, but the rodeo has an off-season and Ben used it to head back to Red Lodge where he raised his own herd—eight kids in ten years. And Ben didn't raise sissies. "He was a strict disciplinarian," one daughter said. "If he ever caught us smoking a cigarette he claimed he'd beat us to death with a fencepost, and we thought he just might have."

Four of the brood—Turk, Marge, Bill, and Alice—became rodeo stars, or as they were introduced at arenas worldwide, the Riding Greenoughs. Among them they would eventually claim 156 rodeo championships.

Turk, a middle child, always wanted to be a cowboy; nothing else mattered. When the 104 Ranch Wild West Show came to Billings, Tom Mix was among the 600 people it employed. But when the show left town there were 601—Turk had a job. But when movies became the rage, Mix left to go to Hollywood, and Wild West shows died. Turk needed a new job. He thought the rodeo was more appealing than ranching, so he hit the circuit, winning his first championship in Livingston before moving on to Pendleton. He kept winning—in Cheyenne, Boston, and Calgary to name a few. But it was in Great Falls where he lost—his heart—to Sally Rand, the famous fan and bubble dancer featured at the 1933 Chicago World's Fair. Even before Turk's divorce was final they were engaged. The couple settled in Red Lodge, but after a few years their bubble burst, and Turk went on to remarry his first wife.

Movies were bigger than ever, especially westerns. Turk's riding skills were in demand in Hollywood, where he met John Wayne while working as a stuntman on a movie. The Duke took a liking to him and he was soon hired as an extra in *Crusades*. He worked the Hollywood circuit just like the rodeo circuit, appearing in movies for Universal, MGM, Paramount, and Republic but became a household name when he appeared in ads for Montgomery Ward, Lee, and Stetson.

Advertising was a family affair for the Greenoughs, and it wasn't unusual to see them promoting all sorts of products. Alice remembers in particular a magazine ad for Camel cigarettes. Fearing her father's reaction, she refused to even hold one, so Camel printed a photo of her astride her horse and placed it next to a pack of cigarettes.

Alice and Marge got their start when they answered an ad for trick and bronc riders, and it wasn't long before they were touring with rodeo shows throughout the West. But their fame didn't come cheap. Marge said that besides the many broken ribs they suffered they both have legs that don't match, and in fact Alice almost had to have one of her legs amputated.

Little did the girls know that the riding skills that Pack Saddle drummed into them as children would carry them across oceans. Royalty met royalty when, Marge, Queen of the Lady Bronc Riders had tea with Queen Mary and King George of England. But her fame didn't stop there. She was invited to Spain to ride fighting bulls. When the revolution broke out she was one of the fortunate ones to get out of the country safely. Even the Australians loved her; she was a superstar down under.

But nowhere was their celebrity status higher than in the United States. At Madison Square Garden—the biggest rodeo of the year—Mayor LaGuardia made it a point to be there to greet the Greenoughs. Even celebrities like Babe Ruth and Sonja Henie—not ones to pass up a photo op—went out of their way to be seen with the rodeo stars. In 1939 Pack Saddle Ben returned to the city he ran away from sixty years before to watch his girls at the Garden.

The Greenough legacy has been passed on. Marge's son Chuck was a

One of the very few businesses in downtown Fromberg, Shirley Smith's bar is hard to miss. Although the exterior is made of stucco and wood, the inside is pure cowboy.

rodeo clown for forty years, which earned him a place in the Cowboy Hall of Fame in Oklahoma; he still does some stuntwork. Deb, Pack Saddle Ben's great-grandson, is a recent national champion. On one wall in the Little Cowboy Bar hangs a picture of Deb and *his* son, dressed in cowboy gear ready to carry on the tradition.

What the memorabilia in Shirley's museum can't tell you about the Greenoughs, she can. "They were my dearest friends and a big part of my life." And that's what the museum is really about—the life and times of Shirley Smith. There's barely a visible inch of wall to hang anything more, but what is there isn't clutter, it's history. From an autographed picture of John Wayne posed with Turk to one of Christian Slater, who appeared at her doorstep, there's a story behind every item—just ask Shirley.

★ *Directions:*

U.S. Highway 310, 38 miles southwest of Billings; exit Interstate 90 at Laurel.

For more information:

Little Cowboy Bar, 406-668-9502.

Madison Buffalo Jump State Park,
Logan

From the road it looks like any of the thousands of cliffs in Montana. But at the base lie the scattered bones of bison, some dating back 2,000 years, some 5 feet underground. This is the Madison Buffalo Jump, a crucial part of Native American life. Their very survival depended on the nondescript cliffs they called pishkuns.

Used from 2,000 until as recently as 200 years ago, the site was most active in the fall when Shoshone and Bannock tribes gathered food for the winter. A tribe would pick its fastest runner, who started the hunt by finding bison and leading them toward the cliffs as women and children watched, giving the event an almost festival-like atmosphere. The runner drove the herd to the edge of the cliff where they fell by the hundreds to their deaths. Those that went over last sometimes survived because their fall was cushioned by those preceding them, but they were finished off with clubs and spears. The lucky few who smelled danger escaped, only to continue the tradition the next year and the next.

The women butchered the bison on the spot, and it was not unusual for a tribe to spend days at the site processing meat (most was dried for winter use) and dressing and tanning hides. Although the natives could get a year's worth of food with this method, it was not only for food that the bison was revered. Not a bit was wasted: the hides provided shelter, robes, moccasins, dresses, and shirts; bones were used for needles and awls; sinew made a strong thread; and the horns became spoons and ladles.

Buffalo jumps are also sites of spiritual vision quests and eagle catching pits in which a man would lie on his back thoroughly camouflaged but with live bait, a rabbit perhaps, on his chest. His arms were free to grab an eagle as it swooped down to nab the bait (the eagle's feathers were crucial to some ceremonies and were highly prized).

This is the business side of the buffalo jump. What you can't see are the miles of open prairie that end abruptly at the cliffs.

Once the Native Americans were introduced to the white man's guns and horses, there was no need for the jumps, and they fell into disuse. At Madison it's hard to imagine how anything could survive a fall off the cliffs, which are about thirty feet high, much less the ensuing tumble down the hillside. This is emphasized even more if you hike the trail that leads to the top; be careful where you put your hands and feet: rattlesnakes are common here.

Although these methods are by today's definition primitive, they were effective and the Native Americans killed only what they needed to survive. In spite of the numbers that were harvested on the annual drives, ironically it was the white man who took the bison to the edge of extinction.

★ *Directions:*
Exit for Madison Buffalo Jump off Interstate 90 between Three Forks and Manhattan.

For more information:
Madison Buffalo Jump has interpretive signs and is open year-round; phone 406-994-4942.

Additional site:

Ulm Pishkun State Park, just southwest of Great Falls off Interstate 15, is one of the largest pishkuns in the country (there are several buffalo jumps in the state but most are inaccessible or on private land). The visitor center is open from Memorial Day to the end of September; hours are from 10 A.M. to 5 P.M. Tours can be scheduled in advance or you can take a self-guided tour from the visitor center; phone 406-866-2217. State park fees apply to both sites.

did you know...

9

In northern Montana, Highway 200 is known as the "loneliest road in America." In the southern part of the state, Charles Kuralt dubbed the Beartooth Highway "the most beautiful road in America."

Egg Mountain, **Choteau**

I t's not hard to imagine that you've gone back in time a hundred years or so. This lush grassy valley at the base of the Rocky Mountain front is home to a small colony of tepees. Pronghorn antelope, elk, and grizzly roam nearby, and the only sound is the wind.

This is "Camposaur," a paleontological research station sitting on what was once Blackfeet land. Blackfeet tepees are the structure of choice because they have proven to be the most wind-resistant type of tent, yet brutal Choteau winds have stripped even one of these structures bare. But the resemblance to a Blackfeet encampment stops there. Shades of modern life appear in the form of solar showers, makeshift horseshoe pits, and an earth-toned mobile home office. The surrounding two-square-mile area is owned by The Nature Conservancy and operated by Bozeman's Museum of the Rockies. Each year from mid-June through late August nearly 600 museum personnel, teachers, and dino buffs dig holes and sift sand in search of bits and pieces of dinosaurs.

The area became a hotbed of prehistoric proportions when some rock hounds, while scouring the area for fossils, came across an immensely important discovery—evidence of dinosaur nesting, specifically the duck-billed maiasaurs. Finally, proof to dispel the widely held notion that dinosaurs were stupid, cold-blooded, and solitary critters. In fact, the maiasaurs—Montana's state fossil whose name means "good mother lizard"—appear to have been intelligent, warm-blooded, social animals that took good care of their young. Here in Egg Mountain are fossilized remains of not just maiasaur young but their eggs as well—the first found anywhere.

Annually, more than 5,000 visitors show up for the daily free tour that takes them to the actual nest site and nearby fossil quarry. The research plot is just part of a much larger area that once was home to 10,000 or more *Maiasaura peeblesorum* dinosaurs. Ash layers suggest that volcanic activity, rapid melting, and subsequent mud flows created

To world-class paleontologists and amateur dinosaur diehards, windswept Camposaur looks like Club Med.

layers of carcass-riddled silt. The huge inland sea that covered much of eastern and central Montana fluctuated over time and created more layers. Plate shifts shoved some layers skyward where glaciers later sheared them, making them accessible today.

In spite of a short excavation season, thousands of fossil bones and related specimens have been unearthed. Egg fragments litter the ground beneath your feet like black confetti. No complete eggs have been found; however, enough related material has been unearthed to tell scientists a great deal about how they were incubated and arranged in the nests. Four nests have been uncovered. Researchers now also know that the young were twelve inches at hatching, that the egg was the size of an ostrich's, and that there were up to eighteen young in a nest. Parents reaching thirty feet long tended to their young until they were old enough to migrate with the herd.

Speculation about the cause of the dinosaurs' downfall continues, but the abundance of petrified dino poop makes it clear that they did not die from bowel impaction. Dinosaur teeth are well preserved, too, and are commonly found here, not surprising considering they had nearly 700 in their mouth, although only several hundred of them were functional. Dung and teeth experts have determined that the maiasaurs were vegetarians.

Guides at Egg Mountain are enthusiastic and have the latest dirt on dinos. They'll readily point out that the stone you just tripped over is a time-traveled dinosaur remnant.

According to guide Peter McNair, "The more we learn, the more we learn how to look." And look they do. From the casually interested to the dino addicted, visitors come from all over the world. Some even drop a good chunk of change to work with the experts and join in on the excavation. Despite the wind, heat, wind, and more wind, people will dig, stepping back eons in time, continuing the transition from dinosaurs to tepees.

★ *Directions:*
12 miles west of Choteau.

For more information:
Museum of the Rockies, 406-994-6618; daily tours at 2 P.M.

Bear Creek Saloon Pig Races,
Bearcreek

Picture it: It's a hot Friday night; the dust in the air is as thick as the country-western music coming from the loudspeakers; you down the last few drops of your beer as the bleachers fill to standing room only. The contestants enter the arena, circling the track before heading toward the starting gate. After the announcer's introductions, a trumpet sounds, a bell rings, and with a squeal they're off. Someone near you yells, "Move it, pig," but you stay put. You couldn't be anywhere else in Montana but Bearcreek.

With about 50 residents, Bearcreek is Montana's smallest incorporated town, but each weekend from Memorial Day through Labor Day the population can swell to more than 500, all due to the Bear Creek Saloon, the town's only business. Here is Bear Creek Downs—since 1989 home to the state's only pig races. Saloon owner Bob ("Pits") DeArmond began the races to counteract a slow tourist season during the 1988 Yellowstone fires. Why races, and especially why pigs? "Small town, short season," he says. "Besides, pigs are easy to train and they run good, much better than the iguanas we once tried."

But bringing home the bacon wasn't always easy. The state board of horse racing got wind of the races and declared them illegal. Bob persisted, doing battle in Helena for months. Finally, the notorious pig racing bill was introduced; four months later HB #443 was passed—Bob and the pigs were back in business, this time as a nonprofit fundraiser.

Betting windows open promptly at 7 P.M. Twelve times a night groups of five piglets led by such porcine celebrities as Makin' Bacon, Miss Piggy, and Nota Hot Dog run like their lives depend on it. Two bucks buys you a spot on the sports pool–style board—"kind of like keno with pigs," Pits tells patrons. The winning pig pays $25, half of

Our winning pig, Justa Wiener, takes the lead and never looks back, leaving Swiney River, Sonic Sow, Jimmy Dean, and Little Pig Man to eat his dust.

each race's pot. The other half goes toward scholarships for Carbon County high school students—more than $36,000 to date.

When Pits and his wife, Lynn, bought the saloon in 1982 it didn't even have a kitchen much less a racetrack. Now customers can down their favorite steak before strolling out back to the balcony overlooking the track that is complete with bleachers, lights, and enclosed walls plastered with local advertising. The focal point of the infield is a gold-painted pig statue that rules over, appropriately, a huge bed of petunias.

It's almost race time. The suspense builds as the little porkers in their brightly colored racing silks mill about the track, prominently sporting sponsors' names on their backs: on any night Ham And Organ might be touting the Bridger Café. The excitement intensifies when the sprinters are ushered to the starting gate by high school kids affectionately known as sowboys. The gate opens and bettors get to their feet to cheer on their favorite entrée. But the losers have nothing to fear; in fact, they live high on the hog—the humane society makes sure of that.

People from all fifty states and dozens of countries have placed bets. Pits and his crew have been featured on national television and in numerous magazine and newspaper articles. They're constantly improving the grounds. "This year we've added a large playground to make the event more of a family affair," Pits says.

Even if you don't win a race you won't go home empty-handed. You'll always have the satisfaction of contributing to a good cause, memories of something uniquely Montana, and, maybe best of all, a plastic souvenir beer cup reminding you that Bear Creek Saloon is "Where Pigs Do Fly."

★ *Directions:*
7 miles east of Red Lodge on Highway 308.

For more information:
Bear Creek Saloon, 406-446-3481.

did you know...

10 Belfry's high school team is the Bats; Belt's, however, is the Huskies, not the Buckles.

Sign reads: We Support the Timber Industry.

Manning Theater, **Hysham**

Dave Manning was a politician, inventor, and doer of good deeds. But to the kids and neighbors in Hysham he was primarily the weekend projectionist at the town's Yucca Theater. Not a big deal really except that he also designed and built the theater. It's not just any small-town movie house—its Santa Fe and art deco style makes it the focal point of Hysham.

When cattleman Charlie Hysham settled in the area at the turn of the century, the goods he ordered that were delivered by rail were tagged "for Hysham." The name stuck. Hysham's population of 500 to 600 hasn't fluctuated much over the past several decades. It had a growth spurt from the early 1920s to the mid-1930s, which accounts for the unusually large amount of deco architecture for a town its size.

It was about that time when Dave Manning returned from the Southwest where he worked as a contractor before starting his own contracting business. He and brother, Jim, constructed the theater around 1931. It was an instant hit. Dave's niece Pat Mysse recalls how much fun it was to be in the projection room while her cousin, David Jr., ran the projector. "I could sit anywhere I wanted to, but I especially liked the balcony." Movie prices ranged from nine cents for kids to forty cents for adults, but this was the depression and it wasn't unheard of for some folks to pay with cream or chickens.

Because the nearest theater was thirty miles east or fifty miles west, the Yucca was usually filled to capacity. "Each week we'd go to the surrounding towns and distribute posters advertising the coming attraction," says Dave's daughter, Shirley. When she was twelve years old, she began to manage the ticket booth. "I would stay in the booth for about three-quarters of the film, but I saw the ends of many great movies." However, some movies she never saw at all; if a patron had a fussy child she would babysit in the booth. (Today she subscribes to a classic movie channel to fill in the blanks.) She also mentions that community and high school

Dave and Jim Manning have indeed left their mark on Hysham. The Yucca Theater is on the National Register of Historic Places.

dances—even the prom—never started until the night's movie was over. And in Hysham the prom was the event of the year—the whole town turned out.

Films were shown on weekends only. The first one, in 1931, was *A Room With A View*—a 1914 classic. *Tillie's Punctured Romance* was the last film to grace the screen, in 1986. The interior of the theater was as magical as the movies. Dave's brother, Jim, had a hand—literally—in decorating the ceiling and walls. He painstakingly textured them with his hands, the knuckles to be exact, then finished them with glitter-laced gold paint.

The theater was a labor of love, giving Dave great satisfaction in seeing others enjoy his movies. But it turns out his real love was politics. In 1933 he decided to run for a seat in the Montana House of Representatives, which he easily won. After eleven years he entered the senate where he served until his retirement at eighty-seven in 1985. He holds the record as the longest serving legislator in the United States—fifty-two continuous years. He was a good man, an honest politician who liked to say that he represented cows, fenceposts, and roads, not just people. This may be why he never had a primary opponent, never lost an election, yet did it all as a Democrat in Republican country. Shirley says, "He always voted for the bill, not the party."

You don't devote that much of your life to something without accumulating tons of mementos. In 1989 Hysham established the Treasure County 89ers Historical Museum and soon dedicated it to Senator Manning. A year later the Manning family donated the theater to the museum, conveniently located across the street. Sylvia Lyndes, president of the historical society, organized his effects for the Manning museum. The resulting Hysham museum "complex" consists of the 89ers building, the theater, and the Manning residence.

Senator Manning annually went to Washington where he met every president as far back as FDR. Photos of him and his wife, Ruth, with Kennedy, Nixon, and Johnson, as well as their signatures, are on display. One room of the residence holds nearly a dozen of Ruth's inaugural gowns, complete with accessories. But it wasn't uncommon for dignitaries to show up on his doorstep as well, and the Manning kids often found politicians in their living room. Shirley says, "When Mike Mansfield showed up at the door looking for my father, we weren't awed, we just took it for granted."

But don't forget Dave was also an inventor. You can see his patents for a boring machine that drilled holes for telephone poles (he personally helped plant the first pole in the state) and a turntable trailer that was used for hauling heavy equipment. He also played a key role in developing an alternate form of energy by storing floodwaters and was instrumental in getting many of Montana's gravel roads paved.

The theater wasn't the only Southwest-style building in Hysham. Mexican migrant workers built five adobe dwellings as temporary housing, which were later used to hold WWII POWs. Unfortunately the only thing left are the photos in the 89ers Museum, where you can find more of Hysham's colorful past such as homesteads, hangings, and a few suspicious fires, one of which burned the better part of a city block.

The Hysham Chamber of Commerce brochure invites you to stay for a day or a lifetime. It's almost as if Dave Manning knew not everyone would be staying. So, as you leave town for the two-mile drive back to the interstate, just remember the road you're on is paved because of Dave.

★ Directions:
North of Interstate 94 halfway between Billings and Miles City.

For more information:
406-342-5452 or 342-5252; the theater is being restored, so call for hours.

St. Marie

I n the 1950s as thousands of tourists came to Montana to visit its many ghost towns, the federal government was busy creating the state's largest one yet. Out on the high plains of Valley County in northeastern Montana sits the hulk of what was once a thriving community of nearly 10,000—larger than most of the state's towns. There, adjacent to the monstrous runway at Glasgow Air Force Base was a typical American town where folks hustled off to work, carted their kids to school, and mowed their lawns. There were schools, churches, a clinic, cinema, and bowling alley—all the amenities of a healthy community. It's still there—everything, that is, except the people.

Driving down its streets suggests a scene from a science fiction movie—you know, the kind where everyone mysteriously disappears. The village is surreal. The airstrip's massive hangars with warning signs adorning its chainlink fence create a foreboding presence. You get the feeling you're being watched, and in fact, you are. One step beyond the No Trespassing signs, and security guards come out of nowhere. In the residential areas, lawns are window high, forests of weeds grow through cracks in the macadam roads, obscuring sidewalks and devouring curbs. Driveways and backyards are barren and playgrounds are eerily lifeless. The only movement is created by the wind.

But it wasn't always like this. The war in Vietnam had created a surge in military demand, and this facility was in the heart of it. The base enjoyed twenty years of growth and prosperity until the war waned. Then, in 1976 when federal budgets were squeezed to their limits, so was the town, and almost overnight the place was empty. Attempts to rebuild the local economy by bringing in AVCO, a munitions-support business, fizzled after a few years. Mountain-Plains/Family Training Center, Inc., a six-state federally funded program aimed at training low-income citizens and welfare recipients was launched. "It was like a college for the underprivileged," says Kathy Steele, one of 198 remaining residents who worked

Location, location, location. 360-acre handyman's special. Really quiet neighborhood, lots of living space, no traffic. Convenient to airport.

there for the ten years it operated. Energy research testing, grass mat manufacturing, television and movie production—more than a dozen businesses in all have given this location a shot. Unfortunately, they've all moved on. Few people could afford to stay, and the town gradually slipped into disrepair.

In the midst of this, Valley County was given stewardship of the entire complex, and two years later the federal government turned over complete ownership. In 1985 developer Pat Kelly bought the holdings—airstrip and all—for just over a half million dollars. His plan was to sell off the housing bit by bit, but his wife, Judy, convinced him to convert the town into a retirement community for military personnel. They named it St. Marie after an infant daughter they lost. The plan was grandiose—maybe too lofty. The eighteen-hole golf course, fitness center, and medical facility he'd promised never materialized. He managed to sell a couple hundred of the 1,200 housing units—some of which were hauled off to other parts of the state. When Judy died, so did the vision of St. Marie, which was sold again in 1996 to a less-scrupulous developer. Within a short time, the new owner had generated enough debt and legal tangles to muddy things for years to come.

There's always speculation about what will become of the base and its adjacent town. The latest is the shuttle scuttle; the word is that NASA plans to eventually develop a fleet of spacecraft capable of launchless takeoffs, just like an airplane. The program, named Venture Star, could be the CPR that revives the town. St. Marie has most of the amenities NASA's looking for: a 13,500-foot airstrip (currently owned by Boeing)— one of the longest anywhere—that was built extra thick to handle Montana winters; the large amount of water needed for cooling the craft, from nearby Fort Peck Lake; and the kind of out-of-the-way location that large government projects salivate over. Then there's the St. Marie infrastructure: 360 acres with water, sewers, power, schools, a church, roads, housing—the whole nine yards—available immediately. Just like its first residents, it's on standby, ready to serve its country once again.

★ *Directions:*
17 miles north of Glasgow on Montana Highway 24.

For more information:
406-524-3156 or 406-524-3150 (after 6 P.M.).

did you know...

You'll find the towns of Ynot, Whoop-Up Trail, and Ubet in Montana—you bet.

Robber's Roost, **Alder**

Think of the worst motel you ever stayed in, then add prostitutes, gambling, and gunfire, and you have an idea of what a night's stay was like at Pete Daly's Place. When he built the stage stop in 1863, Daly's intention was to create a respite for travelers between Bannack and Virginia City. The two-story log structure soon became a regular stop for desperadoes and road agents such as the notorious sheriff Henry Plummer and his band of thugs.

The roost's actual history has been romanticized over the years and a good yarn may have replaced fact. But several tales persist. If you stand in front of the building and look at the verandah, it's easy to believe that Plummer did his diabolical planning here. It wouldn't be a stretch either to imagine that two outlaws were hanged nearby.

The first floor catered to gamblers and the occasional imbiber; upstairs, guests could dance or spend the night—alone or with a female "companion." Bullet holes in the log walls speak loudly of the character of Pete's patrons. Because of this reputation as a hangout for lowlifes, it was dubbed robber's roost.

Customers often paid in gold. Add to this the gold that was heisted, and it's easy to see how the rumor began of a treasure hidden close by. But as the interpretive sign says, "Drive over and pay your respects but please don't dig up the premises trying to locate the cache." Although you may walk around the grounds, changing ownership makes getting inside hit or miss.

Although its colorful patrons are long gone, the building's character remains. It may never make the cover of *Good Housekeeping*, but it has held up as well as most of its tales. If only walls could talk.

★ *Directions:*
Montana Highway 287 north of Virginia City in southwest Montana.

For more information:
Montana State Historical Society, 800-243-9900.

did you know...

12   *Montana is the fourth most seismically active state.*

Hay Bales, **Hobson** *and* **Utica**

E nter Hobson from nearly any direction and you can't help but be impressed by the vast solitude. This is Montana at its big-sky best. In late summer, combines shave the hay fields to a uniform smoothness. In this area rocks and outcroppings stand like monuments against the barren wheatscape and cerulean sky, and any foreign protrusion commands your attention. But the gentle calm of the serene slopes is jolted when you realize that the mesh-fenced plots along the highway silently house the underground missile silos of the U.S. military. On a crisp mid-September day, however, you can easily dismiss them as you travel the back roads around Hobson enjoying a whole other form of protrusion—hay bales.

But while these are no ordinary agricultural artifacts, neither do they pose the mystery of crop circles. Punctuating the draws and benches of the Judith Basin, these byway bales have a message meant to bring a smile and lift a spirit. They are part of Utica Days, a hay bale decorating competition that's been evolving in the Hobson area over the past several years. The twenty-five-mile-long festival could lay claim to being the "largest" anywhere. Just as townfolk in most cities compete when adorning their homes for Christmas, Hobson area ranchers enjoy their own version of seasonal decorating. And each year the competition has become more heated.

Rules allow for a lot of latitude. But there appears to be two constants that guide each entry: they must be made mostly of hay and (apparently) must be accompanied by a bad hay-related pun. In a year rocked by political scandal the opportunities to mock the headlines with takes on *Bale* Clinton and Monica Lewinsk*hay* proved irresistible. But clearly nothing is sacred. A large round bale modified to resemble a swine is labeled "Miss *Hay*ggy." Another set of round bales stacked vertically and spray-painted pink is dubbed "*Straw*berry Milksh*ay*ke." And who couldn't fall in love with the field full of spotted hay puppies labeled "101 *Bale*mations?"

In addition to small rectangular bales, some entrants use big round ones, the kind that's unrolled to feed large herds. But these hay burners are cheap to feed and in fact could win their creator $500.

Since the bale festival is unrelated to any other seasonal event, no holiday is off-limits. So displays featuring signage reading "Be My *Bale*ntwine" and "*Hay* la lu yah" are perfectly at home. Capitalizing on the throngs passing through his district, one inventive political candidate put a "Vote for Kunkel" sign on a solitary bale that, no doubt, everyone unwittingly stopped to look at—we did. And no reverence was lost on the "*Bales* of St. Mary's."

Competition is fierce. Contestants typically wait until the very last minute to complete their works for fear of having their ideas ripped off. Some builders have been ingenious, incorporating mechanization (to create a wagging tail on a round-bale cow) and wooden cut-outs (for horse heads and drivers on a st*hay*ge coach) to embellish their projects. The stage, by the way, passes a road sign directing travelers to *Hay*bson and Utic*hay*.

The gateway to the open-air display is the east end of Hobson's main street, right where it intersects Montana Highway 200. Here you can join the caravan of strawgazers. Like a funeral procession without a destination, strings of cars creep along the road between Hobson and Utica, pausing at pastures to snap a picture or share comments with other gawkers. Additional contenders can be viewed along roads through nearby Stanford and Windham as well.

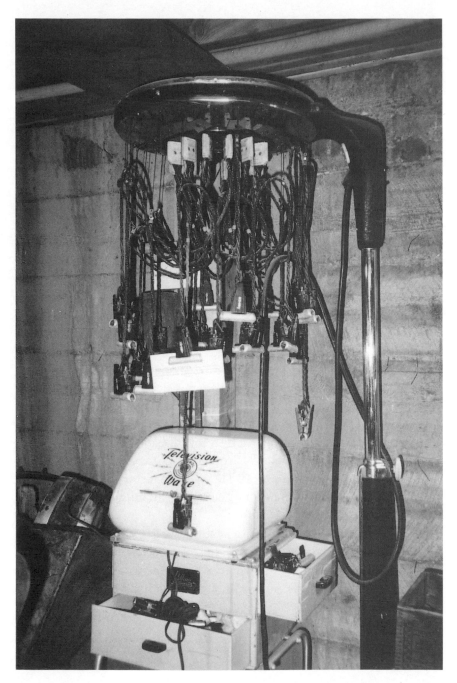

An instrument of torture? A spider milking machine? Jumper cables for a really dead car? Whatever it is, it may be the only one in the state. And Utica's got it.

Zipping through Hobson, however, would be a mistake. Its quaint boulevard sports a selection of displ*hays* for the motorist to enjoy. A local civic group offers a book sale and flea market while some merchants, eager to take advantage of the increased traffic, expand their operating hours on this special weekend. Even a few side street residents have expressed themselves with front lawn hay statements.

Midway between Hobson and Utica a craft show gives one farmstead a carnival-like appearance. Hot dog and hamburger smoke fills the air. At the route's terminus in Utica—population twenty-five—the festivities continue with another bazaar of craftspeople and tented vendors set up midway-style in the community park. Here you can find everything from embroidered Christmas ornaments and hand-painted saws to fajitas and hot dogs. Local ladies have an exhaustive selection of desserts available at a modest price. Within this atmosphere of a church picnic, the slim shoulders of Utica's dirt streets become jammed with cars. Neighbors converge at the few scattered outdoor tables to down a dog and discuss this year's array of straw entrants.

A respite of sorts is the Utica Museum. Providing a little shade and a lot of local color, the museum is housed on two levels and contains some of Utica's cherished memorabilia. An attendant is always available to answer questions, although most every item is clearly labeled. Sometimes, however, an object's inclusion requires an explanation; for example, who is Ted Olsen and why is his hammer on display?

Utica served as a stage stop between Billings and Fort Benton, and its founder John Murphy (originally from Utica, New York) donated the land that formed the town in 1880. The colorful history of Utica includes cattle roundups, Calamity Jane's presence, and an interesting fascination with Will Rogers.

If you want more details before heading out, just pick up the phone and call information. If you're lucky, like we were, you'll get Wendy in Spokane. Her grandmother Mildred Taurman just happens to be a Hobsonian and had all the answers. Now, if that isn't the last straw.

★ *Directions:*
Hobson is in central Montana on U.S. Highway 87/Montana Highway 200 about 80 miles east of Great Falls.

For more information:
406-423-5248.

Orphanage, **Twin Bridges**

Twin Bridges is a tale of two cities. Today it is the quintessential Montana fly fishing town. *Sports Afield* picked it as the best place to catch trout in the world. R. L. Winston Rod, internationally known maker of custom fly rods, is the town's largest employer. It's probably the kind of place that Mormons M. H. and John T. Lott envisioned when they established the town in 1866 and eventually built the bridges that the town is named for.

But across the river stands the neglected reminder of a less idyllic Twin Bridges, a campus that most locals don't even think about other than that it needs work. They also don't pay much attention to the large sign that's been there for 20 years: Historic Complex for Sale, 223 Acres with Beaverhead River Frontage. This is the Montana Children's Center, more commonly known as the orphanage.

Twin Bridges was a major player in the Anaconda Company, shipping copper, gold, silver, and lead from the Tobacco Root Mountains. But as with most small towns in Montana, mining's decline destroyed its financial stability, so the Lotts donated 233 acres to build the orphanage in the hope of boosting the economy—and boost it did. In 1893 the Montana Children's Center became a major source of income for the locals.

Most of the children living in the complex were not orphans in the traditional sense; they were placed here by parents who were unable to take care of them or simply didn't want another mouth to feed. Many were from alcoholic or abusive families. During the Great Depression when unemployment was at its highest, so was enrollment, reaching 300 give or take; later years would see an average of 200. Files in the basement of one government building in Helena were overflowing with written promises from parents to their children, saying they would come back for them, which of course they never did. By the time it closed in 1975, some 6,000 children might have been made that same promise.

Almost all of the kids had at least one living parent. Bill Hanley and his older brother, for instance, were taken to the orphanage when their father was sent to prison and their mother couldn't care for all four sons. He was four years old when he arrived and stayed until he was seventeen. In those thirteen years he saw his mother only six times, and that was only when his stepfather came to Twin Bridges to fish on the Beaverhead.

Bill has mixed memories. He recalls how every humanitarian organization made the orphanage their cause at Christmas, the Anaconda Company and the Elks Lodge two of the larger ones. "It was better than any Christmas we would have had at home—each kid got ten to fifteen gifts." But that once a year treat was hardly worth feeling too kindly about the remaining 364 days. His worst memory (besides weeding the four-acre garden) was that it seemed like the doctors were operating under a quota to remove tonsils. "We came to dread March every year, when about thirty kids would have their tonsils removed." But even more, he hated the dining hall's dinner bell. "The bell would ring, we'd sit. When it rang again, we'd say grace. Another bell, we'd eat. Another bell, we'd stop."

Throughout campus boys and girls were segregated by sex and age; they referred to the administration building as the Great Wall of China.

The original building set the stage for the orphanage complex. It housed a dining room, laundry, washroom, and showers on the first floor. Upstairs were a nursery, two school rooms, teachers' living quarters, and an office. The third floor had dorms and the matron's office. In addition to storage, the attic housed a playroom and a gym.

Even in the cafeteria the boys would be at one end and the girls would be at the other and, according to Bill, "that infernal woman with the bell was in the middle."

Discipline was severe. Bill says he had many rulers broken over his head, although everyone was treated equally—not necessarily fairly, but equally. He pooh-poohs those residents who claim they were beaten or stripped naked, and says these were fantasies or rumors that helped the kids get through the loneliness that attacked everyone at one time or another. He doesn't have any genuinely bad feelings about the orphanage and says that almost all of the youngsters were better off than if they had been left at home. Even so, that didn't stop them from running away; almost everyone ran away at some time. Bill tried at least three or four times—"sometimes because you were mad at your parents or sometimes mad at the orphanage. When you came back you were really punished." Offenders were put in a locker room where they might spend three or four days on rations—the administration's version of a jail.

Maxine Thompson, who lived here from 1949 to 1956 remembers running away about five times. "We had no plan; we just left. Once we got as far as Sheridan [nine miles away], which took all night." She thinks that they weren't as much running away from the orphanage as they were trying to get back home.

Maxine almost fondly remembers that they could go to more places than a lot of other kids. "Through the efforts of altruistic groups we were taken on field trips and such—one group even went to Disneyland. Our parents couldn't or wouldn't have done that for us."

Everyone was allowed one hour under strict observation on Sundays for visiting. They would gather in front of the "castle" (administration building), in most cases the only time and place brothers and sisters could see each other. Reward for the well behaved was a trip across the bridge into town for a movie. But Maxine was mischievous, and at least once a month, she had to stay back and wash the hospital windows as punishment. "I missed an awful lot of movies, but nobody ever beat me. I have good memories." But she also says, "I don't care if I ever go back there again, it's so run down."

The orphanage was self-sustaining, a small community where the residents were taught to be proficient in life skills. It had its own hospital and dentist, a fully equipped gym, laundry, the third largest swimming pool in Montana, its own basketball and baseball teams, and the orphanage band (in the town's museum is a photo of the band along with the trumpet that is held by a student in the photo). A dairy and a farm with four acres of crops and pigs, chickens, and cows allowed the orphans to learn animal husbandry, butchering, and breeding. Domestic skills weren't ignored either; girls worked in the bake shop and were taught to make all their own clothing, boys spent their time in the woodworking and shoe repair shops. Materialistically, the children wanted for nothing, and all the "graduates" agree that this learned work ethic was helpful later in life when they got out into the real world and needed jobs.

Maxine recalls, "We did have a lot there—more than a lot of other kids had. But the one thing we didn't have was love, something so many people take for granted. We all swore we'd never allow our children to end up in an orphanage."

All the kids went to grade school on the premises even though there was one in town, but when they were high school age, they joined the other kids in Twin Bridges. At sixteen or seventeen they were placed locally as ranch hands, some forming lasting relationships with their employers but few being adopted because they were now too old (once they reached 18 they had to leave the orphanage).

Over the years the complex became less of an orphanage and more of a detention home for problem and reservation kids (eighty percent were Native Americans in the late 1950s). Bill says, "There were a lot of drugs here then. When administrators found kids sniffing glue in the willow trees along the river, their solution was to cut down the trees."

But the orphanage held secrets that didn't emerge until the 1990s when several of the alumni who were trying to find their roots visited the cemetery, where it was rumored that children were buried in unmarked graves. As orphans these same people were responsible for maintaining the gravesites, which were nothing more than a metal tag or a board with a number on it, but no names. They found that nearly 103 orphans had succumbed to the flu epidemic from 1918 to 1921, sometimes three and four dying in a day, sometimes several dumped into the same grave. People were terrified of touching the bodies, so everything was done quickly and quietly without fanfare or mourning. The other orphans were told that the dead were "taken away," which indeed they were, to the state plot on the hill overlooking town and the orphanage. Headed by David Gilligan of Missoula, the alumni managed to identify ninety-eight of these victims and created a memorial listing them—eight names are still unaccounted for.

Today the site is rife with broken windows, leaking roofs, major asbestos problems, and overall neglect. The only residents now are pigeons.

Although Bill has organized two reunions that were attended by nearly 200 alumni from all 50 states and Puerto Rico, he doubts there will ever be another large get-together again. "So many people were depressed at the condition that the present owner has caused through neglect that they don't want to come back." But some have never left: about twelve of the home children still live in the valley and a few others are looking for retirement property. Bill boasts that of the graduates one man was responsible for developing the laptop computer, one was an international teacher, one served and died on the *Arizona* in Pearl Harbor. He says, "Basically they all turned out well—*because* of the orphanage, not in spite of it."

An annual event in Twin Bridges, Floating Floatilla and Fish Fantasies, raises money to support the town's museum, which showcases what is left of the orphanage and its history. The orphanage ceased to exist after eighty-two years. Although its structures are neglected and in need of major repair, the memories of those who have passed through its halls will last forever.

★ *Directions:*
In southwest Montana about 50 miles south of Butte on Montana Highway 41.

For more information:
Joy Day, Twin Bridges Historical Association, P.O. Box 227, Twin Bridges, MT 59754; phone 406-684-5701.

Sign reads: Judith Gap National Forest, Replanted 1998.

Pompeys Pillar National Historic Landmark, **Pompeys Pillar**

Interstate 90 passes less than a mile from Pompeys Pillar, but for some people zipping along the highway that's too far. And that's a shame, because just north of here on the rock outcrop is William Roger Clark's signature, the only remaining physical evidence of the Lewis and Clark Expedition. It's at the pillar where you can be assured of standing in Clark's footsteps—more than 50,000 people have.

The 117-foot-high sandstone butte lies along the Yellowstone River, where it serves as a distinctive landmark, which is why on July 25, 1806, Clark chose to put his name here on his return trip (Lewis was taking a northern route). But he certainly wasn't the first to leave his mark. For 5,000 years the Indians used this site, which the Crow called "Where the Mountain Lion Lies," as a story rock, somewhat like a modern day newspaper or bulletin board. They left petroglyphs to warn of danger or advertise good hunting spots. Nor was Clark the first white man to pass through here; writings in Antoine Larocque's (a French fur trader) journal mention his passing the tower a year earlier.

Clark was inspired by the view and the herds of elk and bison that could be seen from the top of the rock. He decided to name the spot Pompey's Tower, after Sacagawea's son, Baptiste, whom he nicknamed Pomp (Shoshone for "little chief"). Editor Nicholas Biddle took the liberty of changing the name to Pompeys Pillar in 1814 when Clark's journals were published. In 1998 a citizens group, trying to right this as well as other geographic wrongs, launched a campaign to change the name back to Pompeys Tower. As of this writing it remains Pillar.

For nearly sixty miles it was the only point where the river could be easily accessed and traversed from either shore. Consequently, herds of bison and elk regularly funneled through this natural ford, which in

Clark's signature is protected from further erosion with a clear covering. To avoid glare, Ken Burns filmed a replica on display in the visitor center for his PBS Lewis and Clark documentary.

turn attracted Indians, then later trappers and frontiersmen, who took advantage of this corridor to easily harvest the game.

As the West developed, fur traders crossed here as did homesteaders, missionaries, and the cavalry. In fact, from the top of the pillar you can see where General Custer camped in 1873, about a mile north. Three years later Colonel John Gibbon came through on his way to the Bighorn battle, and some of his men left their signatures here as well.

This was a stopping point for steamship traffic, most notably the *Josephine,* piloted by Captain Grant Marsh, who scratched the ship's name into the pillar in 1875. Less than ten years later, the railroad came through. Many of the construction crew added their names to the pillar, and a few, realizing the value of Clark's signature, took measures to protect it with a screened covering. When automobiles arrived, a bridge was built. As one of the last remaining three-span bridges in Montana, recent plans to tear it down have met such resistance that it has been decided to convert it to a footbridge. A new auto bridge will be constructed nearby.

There's a history to the rock besides the one written on it. It went through a succession of owners before it reached its current status as

National Historic Landmark. The Crow owned the land first. In 1906 it was passed on to the Macer family by way of an Indian homesteading allotment. Martin Tschida bought it in 1924, then sold it to the Foote family thirty years later. While under Foote ownership it was made a state monument, and in 1991 the Bureau of Land Management became the pillar's present owner.

The outcrop itself has not changed much; Clark surely would recognize it, but he'd have a much easier time of getting to the top by using the boardwalks and stairs that pass close by the petroglyphs and signatures. As you look at Clark's signature from the boardwalk at eye level, you realize that something doesn't quite add up—erosion makes him seem a lot taller than he was. What he could easily reach in 1806 is now ten feet off the ground.

What Clark wouldn't recognize is the gravel parking lot, pit toilets, and visitor center, where if you're lucky you might meet interpretive guide John Phillips, who often dresses in period attire and looks very much the part. He will give you details about the pillar that you won't find in any brochure or book, and make it sound as though it all happened just last week.

From the lookout on top of the pillar, you can almost hear the wolves and see the massive herds of bison and elk that impressed Clark so much he included them in his journals.

It's tough to travel anywhere in Montana without coming across something that was named after Lewis and/or Clark: county, town, cavern, bird, river, and more than one motel. Ironically, the one place that isn't named for him, is best known because it bears his name.

★ Directions:
Pompeys Pillar exit off Interstate 90, 30 miles northeast of Billings.

For more information:
Pompeys Pillar, 406-875-2233.

did you know...

13 Home to the world famous Yogo sapphires, Montana's official nickname is the Treasure State, not the Big Sky State; unofficially it's Big Sky Country.

Malmborg School,
Gallatin County

T he scenery from Interstate 90 between Bozeman and Livingston
is quintessentially Montana—pristine meadows, distant white-
capped mountains, rolling grasslands. Sandhill cranes nest in the
wetland meadows, and moose and elk are not uncommon here. It's easy
to see why you might not notice the unusual-looking dull red house just
off the highway. But take a closer look, and you'll find that it's not a
house but a school; in fact, it's the last of its kind in the United States: a
functioning octagonal one-room schoolhouse.

The Malmborg School has been around for nearly 100 years, yet no
one knows for certain why it's octagonal. Some historians speculate that
it has to do with lighting, and it does feel more open inside than a traditional four-walled structure, but windows are on one side of the building
only, and the less scenic side at that. It stands pretty much the same as it
did after it was built in 1905 (the bell tower has been removed because of
a leaky roof, and some of the hardwood flooring is being replaced). Six
two-bay stables accommodated the horses students rode to school each
day. Today the issue of horses at school has come up, but liability pre-
vents them on the grounds unless they're fenced off. Instead, kids—all
eight of them—arrive by bike, on foot, or by parent power.

Beulah Hagerman, the school's clerk, is a Malmborg alumna, as are
her father, her three children, and one grandson. Enrollment hasn't
changed much for the kindergarten through eighth grade facility; in the
past century it has ranged from one to twenty-one students, the average
about 10. Teachers come and go, as well, with one person teaching all
the grades. Turnover is every two to three years, although Beulah remembers one teacher being there for nine years.

The old chalkboard still gets its share of use, but three computers
with Internet access and a television with a VCR command the kids'

The building's only windows face south, whether for maximum light or to help heat the building in the winter, no one knows for sure.

attention. In addition to the ABCs running along the top of the wall, a Self-Affirmation Chart tells you the student body is very 1990s. No longer do students have to haul firewood for heat, and outhouses have thankfully given way to indoor plumbing. Beulah remembers when the pipes froze one winter and everyone had to pack in water. She says that during a severe winter it was too hard for the teacher to get to school every day, so she moved into the cloakroom.

In 1997 a suggestion to close the school created such an uproar that it was dropped—at least for the time being. Arguments that students don't get the proper education were countered with testimonials from the kids themselves, who like the individual attention they can't get in a larger classroom. Here students help students, although it may seem strange at first to see a six-foot eighth grader towering over a small fry who just started kindergarten.

There's a sense of community in the small school: teachers know the kids and their families intimately, all the parents are involved in school activities, and it's hard for a student to misbehave and hide behind the coattails of someone else. After the kids finish eighth grade they transfer to high school in Bozeman, but even though they've been prepared for it, it still comes as a bit of a shock to find themselves sharing a graduating class of nearly 500.

When Olaf Malmborg donated the land for the school some dozen miles out of Bozeman, he never suspected it could be in the way of Gallatin County's rapid growth. So even though it has enjoyed relative solitude for the past 100 years, who knows how long it can hold off becoming nothing more than a snapshot in a photo album.

★ *Directions:*
Jackson Creek exit off Interstate 90 east of Bozeman.

Bear Paw Battlefield, **Chinook**

It's strangely quiet; only a meadowlark's song punctuates the still-
ness. This almost eerie silence belies the battle that took place here
more than 120 years ago. Beyond the parking lot rolling grassland
spreads for miles, and not a tree can be seen. What happened here was
the culmination of a series of tragedies that represents the blackest mark
against the white man in his persecution of the Indian. But the battle of
the Bear Paw was more than just soldier against Indian, much more.

For hundreds of years the Nez Perce lived in the beautiful Wallowa
Valley near the junction of Oregon, Idaho, and Washington. They were a
peaceful tribe, known for their friendliness toward the white man. Chief
Joseph, their leader, whose main job was to take care of women, children, and the elderly, was diplomatic and wise, and the tribe looked to
him in other ways as well. As throughout the West, Indian land was
constantly encroached upon by white settlers, and the Wallowa Valley
was no exception. In 1855 pioneers moved in, and since there wasn't
enough room for both cultures, the government asked the Indians to give
up some of their land and move to a reservation. It wasn't the best situa-
tion, but it allowed Chief Joseph and his people to stay in their beloved
valley.

But a few years later gold was discovered. Now fortune hunters came
in droves, and in 1863 the reservation was cut back to one-quarter its
initial size. They were ordered onto the smaller reservation and given
only three weeks to comply. This did not sit well with the five bands, and
when they refused to sign the new treaty they became known as the non-
treaty tribes.

In addition to gold, this was prime grazing land, and the encroaching
settlers wanted it. Against government orders, they claimed the land even
though Washington ordered them to leave; in fact, in defiance, more moved
in. Through a lot of governmental mismanagement, a new act again
opened the area to homesteaders, and the Nez Perce were harassed in the

hope that they would leave, but now Chief Joseph refused to give up the Wallowa—this was their home.

The government finally ordered the Nez Perce to leave and go to a designated reservation within a reasonable time. What Washington really meant was immediately, but it was winter and the tribe couldn't move its herds, and asked to stay. This dragged on, and in spring the federal officials got fed up and threw a tribal leader into jail; the rest finally gave in and agreed to leave within the month.

What started as a peaceful departure turned ugly when a young Nez Perce was taunted into avenging his father's murder at the hands of a white man years before. In true military fashion troops were called in from all over the country because they feared a major Indian uprising like the previous year at the Bighorn. Thus began a series of clashes fueled by miscommunication and misunderstanding. As the retreating Nez Perce tried to avoid confrontation, the pursuing cavalry created battles and outbreaks at every turn but were always outsmarted in large part because of Chief Joseph's leadership. He was credited as being a military genius, and in many ways he was, but adding to his image were the mistakes made by the army. Additionally, the Nez Perce had a fierce

Holes that once anchored an interpretive sign now make a convenient holder for cigarette offerings. Tobacco is traditionally left to thank the tribe for what they went through.

protection of their homeland and people, giving them incredible courage, and they knew the rugged landscape better than the pursuing cavalry did.

When Chief Joseph's band sought safety in White Bird Canyon, Captain David Perry followed. They moved on to Clearwater River where General O. O. Howard caught up with them (he was to dog them relentlessly). Tribe members raided Howard's camp, stopping his advance when they ran his horses and pack animals off. They arrived in the Big Hole Valley near Wisdom, certain that Howard's troops were a couple of days behind. Hoping to rest they set up camp, unaware that Colonel John Gibbon was also in pursuit. Their leisure in the Big Hole cost them dearly; the effects would be felt months later at Bear Paw.

Gibbon's troops surprised the Nez Perce with an early morning attack on their sleeping village. It was then that Chief Joseph determined the white man would never leave them alone and decided to head to southeastern Montana where they could meet up with their friends, the Crow. Their best course, he felt, was to head east through Yellowstone. Traversing the relatively new park, they took a party of sightseers hostage that were eventually allowed to escape.

They left the east side of the park and found that their former allies, the Crow, were now scouts for the cavalry, and they, too, became foes. So Chief Joseph decided they should go to Canada where they could find safety with Sitting Bull and the Sioux. But they also encountered a new cavalry enemy—Colonel Samuel Sturgis at Canyon Creek just north of Laurel. Chief Joseph's men fended him off and the tribe moved on, crossing the Missouri River at Cow Island where they helped themselves to supplies at a poorly manned army depot.

Sporadic skirmishes interrupted the journey from the Missouri to Bear Paw, including an encounter with a small band of soldiers from Fort Benton. Nearly four months into their flight out of the Wallowa Valley, Chief Joseph and his people were becoming weary, horses were weak, and supplies were low. Bear Paw was just 30 miles from Canada, and the tribe felt there was enough distance between themselves and the pursuing Howard to pause and rest. Again, they were wrong.

Technology caught up with them at Bear Paw. Colonel Nelson Miles, informed of Chief Joseph's location via telegraph, immediately left Fort Keogh and advanced toward the Indian camp. Chief Joseph had no idea Miles was so near. Knowing how poorly Sturgis had performed, and how badly Howard had failed, Miles saw a golden opportunity to make a name for himself—stopping Chief Joseph became his mission. He arrived at Bear Paw with a fresh band of men and a complement of Cheyenne scouts.

Nez Perce lookouts knew something was up when they saw buffalo stampeding but knew it couldn't be Howard. It was only when another scout warned them by waving a blanket that they found out that Miles was approaching. What followed was the battle at Bear Paw, September 30, 1877. Once Miles began his attack, things kept getting worse for the Nez Perce. An unusually early blizzard dumped five inches of snow. Having left their tepees at the Big Hole, and with nothing more than a few blankets for shelter, they used knives and sticks to scrape out pits in the sides of the hills. There was little food and the only available water had to be gotten from the nearby stream at night. The 1,300-mile trek had taken its toll on the tribe's horse herd, with many going lame or dying along the way. Miles knew that if he could separate the horses from the band, he could eliminate their means of escape, and took advantage of the blizzard to do so. The poor visibility also cost the Nez Perce one of their leaders when Chief Lean Elk was accidentally shot by one of his own men.

Determined to end the battle before Howard arrived and take all the credit for Chief Joseph's capture, Miles hoisted the white flag but took Chief Joseph captive when he came to negotiate an honorable surrender. Miles had him chained and thrown outside with the horses; meanwhile, one of Miles's men was captured by the Nez Perce, who gave him a blanket and what little shelter they had, allowed him to keep his firearm, and fed him. The next day Chief Joseph was returned to his camp in exchange for the soldier.

After several more days of fighting, Howard finally showed up, and Chief Joseph realized that for the good of his people he had to surrender. While he was discussing terms with Howard and Miles, Chief Looking Glass thought he saw the Sioux coming from Canada to help them. He stood up in the rifle pit he was manning to get a better view, but was gunned down by a cavalry sharpshooter. Thoroughly defeated, Chief Joseph and his tribe were sent off to reservation land in Oklahoma where they spent the next eight years trying to get back to Oregon. They were finally allowed to settle in Washington on the Colville reservation, but Chief Joseph was never permitted to return to his homeland, the Wallowa.

In 1925 and again in 1932, L. V. McWhorter walked the battleground with survivors Chief White Hawk, Black Eagle, and Many Wounds, who helped him document what happened here. A self-guided walking tour has markers to indicate where Chief Joseph surrendered and where leaders were slain. Clumps of feathers, tobacco plugs, sweet grass—even a baseball cap and bandanna—left by visitors to pay their respects adorn the site where the Nez Perce suffered serious losses.

Now harriers guard the battlefield, their nesting place, and Swainson's hawks soar effortlessly above the interpretive signs. The silence is fittingly reverent. Although the words of Chief Joseph's surrender have been printed countless times, they bear repeating: "It is cold and we have no blankets. The little children are freezing to death. My people, some of them, have run away to the hills, and have no blankets, no food; no one knows where they are—perhaps freezing to death. I want to have time to look for my children and see how many I can find. Maybe I shall find them among the dead. Hear me, my chiefs. I am tired; my heart is sick and sad. From where the sun now stands, I will fight no more forever."

★ *Directions:*
17 miles south of Chinook, off U. S. Highway 2.

For more information:
Nez Perce National Historic Park, Bear Paw Battlefield, 406-357-3130.

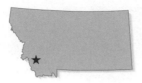

Crystal Park, **Wise River**

I t's like a mecca, attracting people from everywhere who hope to find enlightenment . . . or at least a pretty rock or two. One couple drove 170 miles from Idaho Falls, another came from Kalispell, and yet another from Harlowton to this mountain in the middle of the Big Hole Valley. Their destination—Crystal Park. Set in some of the most sensational scenery in Montana, it's hard to decide whether to look at the landscape or pick up your gear and head for the hill, but the crystals beckon and you put off land-watching until later.

Although the park's interpretive signs go into detail about its treasures, in a nutshell you'll find quartz crystals that were formed about 68 millions years ago when molten granite cooled. The most common ones are hexagonal prisms ranging from clear to cloudy to gray and purple, also known as amethyst. They're found in singles, pairs, and clusters, some as tiny as a carpet tack and others up to six inches.

Rumor has it that the first crystals were found by elk hunters who noticed sparkly rocks in the roots of fallen trees. Today 30 to 40 acres of the 200-acre park are open to recreational rock hounds. But before you charge up the mountainside, take a minute to read the Crystal Tips board for safety suggestions and pointers on how to dig. The decomposed granite is like coarse sand, so you don't need expensive equipment. One father, his little girl in tow, carried a pink-and-yellow plastic Easter bunny pail— and they probably did just fine with it. For more serious digging, a small shovel or garden trowel is a must. Some seasoned diggers wouldn't think of leaving their sifting screen ($^1/_4$-inch mesh) at home, but be advised, no mechanical devices are allowed.

Digging has its hazards; the same properties that make it easy to dig are also responsible for making the soil unstable, and cave-ins are a problem. But unstable soil could be the least of your problems if you don't come prepared with sunblock, insect repellent (mosquitoes can be voracious), hat, and a light jacket—after all, this is Montana and snow and

When rock hounds get together, the conversation always leans toward the day's find. Choice specimens can fetch from $100 to $1,000 or more, but don't quit your job, these are rare.

cool weather are not unheard of in the middle of summer. Just remember, what goes up must come back with you—pack it up, pack it down.

How do you know where to look? "It's real scientific," chuckles Don DeShaw. "You pick a spot and start digging. One to two feet down is best." And he should know. He and his wife, Marla, are avid rock hounds who have been perched on the mountain digging and sifting since 7 A.M.—seven hours ago. Typical of the people here, the Harlowton couple has turned sod all over the state for arrowheads, agates, gold, fossils, and dinosaur bones. But not for profit, "we just love rocks and minerals." Marla is plopped in the middle of their digging pit warding off the sun with a baseball cap, sunglasses, and a sheet tucked under the cap that makes her look like Lawrence of Arabia. She has sifted nearly half a ton of soil using two paper plates with holes punched in the bottoms. But her labor has had its rewards—for their 20th wedding anniversary Don had earrings made out of sapphires he hounded.

Rock hounds have been making the pilgrimage to the mountain since 1987 but only between mid-May and the end of September, depending on snow. Call ahead to find out road conditions if you get the digging itch during the off-season. There's no charge to dig or to use the park's picnic facilities or interpretive trail. No camping is allowed on-site, but there are plenty of campgrounds in the area.

After a full day of digging, within minutes of packing up your gear, you can be back at your campsite washing down the dirt with a glass of whatever it is you wash dirt down with. Sit back, prop your feet up, and enjoy the scenery—it just doesn't get much better than this.

★ *Directions:*
Pioneer Mountains National Scenic Byway, 20 miles south of Wise River.

For more information:
The barrier-free park is jointly maintained by the USDA Forest Service and the Butte Mineral and Gem Club. Phone Beaverhead National Forest, Dillon Ranger Station, 406-683-3900.

Scene Along the Way

Cowboy Boots, **Miles City**

Some people sell them at yard sales, some make them into bird houses, and some folks just throw them away, but Harry Landers tops off his fenceposts with them—cowboy boots, that is.

The idea came to Harry nearly twenty years ago when he saw a similar fence in Nebraska. He rounded up used boots from family and friends, and a landmark was born; they've become a reference point for motorists driving between Broadus and Miles City. People who come to see them frequently leave piles of boots in son Jeff's driveway. As a result, he now has more boots than posts with plenty of spares to replace those that weather. More than 300 boots cover a mile's worth of fence—that's a lot of barefoot cowboys.

★ *Directions:*
About 5 miles south of Miles City on Montana Highway 59; you can't miss them.

Big Ice Cave, **Pryor**

The Pryor Mountains have always been a special place: they're sacred to the Crow tribe, outdoor enthusiasts are drawn to them, and they're such an important part of Pat Pierson's life that he named his son Pryor. As a national forest geologist Pat can talk about the Pryors for hours, but ask him about the ice caves and he really opens up.

Although the Pryors are riddled with caves—the best documented are Big, Little, Red, Pryor, and Crater—only the Big is accessible via a paved path. The caves lie in the Custer National Forest about fifty miles south of Billings, and like most everything else in Montana, they have a history. Legend has it that the Big Ice Cave, discovered in 1888, was a hideout for local outlaw Teton Jackson. Another story suggests that it was used by Native Americans to preserve meat, giving them year-round access to their game. For years the only way to get there was by horse, which on many days is still probably not a bad idea because the road can be gumbo. Even on a dry day with clear skies, it's best to call ahead for road conditions.

The Pryors were once the bottom of a shallow ocean, which accounts for the predominant Madison limestone, a carbonate-type rock. During the mountain-building period, the seabed was thrust upward, creating the Pryor Mountains. Cave making is an ongoing process: precipitation filters through the forest litter where it becomes acidic; it then finds its way through fissures and dissolves the underground limestone layers—a cave is formed.

No surprise there but what accounts for the year-round ice? It's a combination of the cave's shape, constant seepage from above, the insulating properties of the surrounding soil, and cold air displacing warmer air. In short, the warm air in the cave rises and escapes; cold air settles and is trapped. Additionally, the cave entrances face northeast, thus avoiding solar exposure. Seasonal changes do occur inside; depending on when you visit you might see an ice column, formed by the merging of a stalac-

Stay on the boardwalk and do not enter the cave. The best way to see it is from the safety of the platform with a flashlight in hand.

tite and stalagmite. In the Big Ice Cave, the floor ice is usually about six feet thick; the interior is nearly the size of a high school gym.

People come from all over the world to study the nearby 3.4-billion-year-old Beartooth Mountains, many of them making it a point to visit the caves as well. The Forest Service used to provide tours until they became the victims of budget cuts. "We used to guide upwards of 150 people a day on holiday weekends," Pat remarks. Now access is limited to the boardwalk at the entrance—"with good reason," he adds, "because the danger factor is enormous. There's a hole that when we'd drop an ice chip down, it would clink for a long time. Anyone falling down there would become a permanent part of the mountain."

But there's more to the caves than rock and ice; they've held a special place in Crow life since 4,000 B.C. Natural springs, a moderate climate, and a wealth of wildlife made the basin a paradise. The natives called the Pryors the Arrow Mountains because of the abundance of chert, which they used for arrowheads. Fossil remains in sinks (a surface depression caused by a collapsed cave) show evidence of grizzlies, wolves, elk, bison, and even camels. The caves were used as dwellings and shelter during battle.

But the Crow were not alone. Also living in the caves were the Little People. Crow historian Lawrence Flat Lip explains that according to Indian legend, "the Little People are a race of small people that are the very energies that helped the Crow throughout time. They were here for thousands of years before the natives and are responsible for giving us arrowheads." There are three kinds, all with superhuman strength: pure spirits; pure flesh; and half spirit, half flesh. All could morph, and it is said they lived in the rock walls of the caves. Believers and nonbelievers alike have seen them. Some say that when the railroad came through, the Little People left, but Lawrence assures us they're still here. "When you think you see something moving out of the corner of your eye, but there's nothing there, it's probably them."

Although the Little People can be mischievous, they would never damage the caves the way some "big people" have. "Sadly, vandalism has become a real problem. The caves are a nonrenewable resource and should be treated with respect," Pat says. Obey the signs, take only photographs—follow the zero-impact philosophy when in cave country. Keep in mind that access to the caves crosses Indian land and leaving the road is forbidden. Because of the area's fragile ecosystem this is always a good policy. If you visit the area you'll discover that the Pryors are indeed a special place—please keep them that way.

★ *Directions:*
About 50 miles south of Billings in the Pryor Mountains.

For more information:
Beartooth Ranger District, 404-446-2103.

Steer Montana, **Baker**

Texans like to think they have the biggest of everything, but when it comes to cattle, the truth is, they don't. Baker, Montana, has the world's largest steer—it says so on a postcard, so it must be true. Better yet, go see for yourself. Steer Montana (his real name) weighed 3,980 pounds. That's more than the combined weight of the entire starting offense for the Denver Broncos (or Green Bay Packers, depending on your loyalty). Picture a steer on one end of a seesaw and eleven husky guys on the other, and you have a good idea of just how big this animal was.

Unlike many such roadside America attractions, this creature isn't made of concrete and doesn't grace the entrance to a diner or gift shop—it lives in the town's museum under glass, taking up the better part of an entire room. Steer Montana, or "Steer," for short, was born March 23, 1923, and grew to old age in fifteen years and four months. From snout to rump he was ten feet four inches and towered over his pasture pals at six feet (taxidermy has cost him an inch).

Although Steer is the main draw, the O'Fallon Historical Museum has more to offer than most small-town museums. For starters, it's housed in five buildings, one of which was the original jail. Most exhibits have period clothing, but here the traditional wedding gown is navy blue, "to serve double duty for a wedding and possibly a funeral," says curator Lora Heyen. Instead of the usual crazy quilt, you'll find a crazy quilt dressing gown and a flapper dress with hand-beaded fringe. The friendship quilt here is called a suggan, which has 144 names—including one dog and one saddle horse—stitched into the blocks that are pieced-together Bull Durham tobacco sacks. It cost $1 to put your name on it; the proceeds went toward buying school supplies. The whole quilt is stitched in red because "that's the only color they could get here," says Lora. She points out the nearby human hair necklace and adds that women's hair was used for crosshairs in rifle scopes during World War II. In the building across the street even the vehicles are unusual. You can see the Yellow

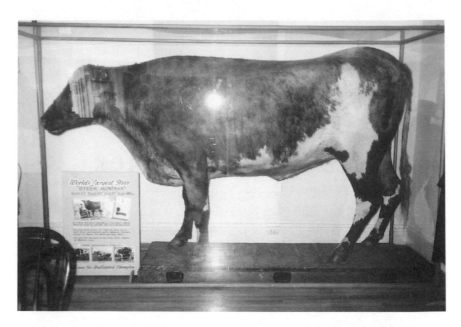

Unofficially topping out at 4,420 pounds, Steer Montana shared the barn with his siblings, Bulgy and Spot, who at 3,000 pounds plus, were no slouches at the feed bin.

Fellow grain thresher made in Peoria, Illinois. The company most likely went out of business because their implements were made of wood and frequently caught fire during use.

But sometimes it's the most nondescript item that has the most interesting story. That's certainly true of the jar of grasshoppers tucked into a corner of a glass display case in building number three—the tool and dinosaur bone building. Containing 1,850 grasshoppers from 1938 (they're dead), the jar is symbolic of a "real bad year," to put it mildly. The jar's contents were removed from just one bundle of rye. According to the homemade photo album that chronicles their invasion, the summer of 1938 held hope for a community that had lost crop after crop from hail and drought. But this year had a wet spring, and the crop looked good. That is, until July 2. The townspeople noticed clouds on the horizon that they thought were prairie fires but were instead millions of hungry grasshoppers that droned like a prop plane and landed with such force they sounded like hailstones on the windows. They ate clothing off washlines, leaving only double seams behind, and pitchforks had to be stored with their handles stuck in bales. Grasshoppers four feet deep in places made the going slick and more than just a bit smelly; road plows were called in to clear them away. It's said they even derailed trains. The chickens thought their ship came in, but even they became frustrated after a day or so. What crops could be salvaged were harvested early to keep them from the ravenous hoppers, but it was a disastrous year for Baker.

Lora says new donations arrive faster than she can find a place for them, but recently she was put to the test when Steer Montana's fully assembled bones arrived. Other museums may have dinosaur skeletons on display, but only Baker has the inside story on Steer Montana.

★ *Directions:*
Baker is on U.S. Highway 12 in eastern Montana; the museum is two blocks off Main Street on the south side of town.

For more information:
O'Fallon Historical Museum, 406-778-3265; open Tuesday through Friday and Sunday, 9 A.M. to 12 noon and 1 to 5 P.M.

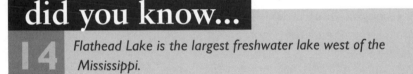

did you know...

14 *Flathead Lake is the largest freshwater lake west of the Mississippi.*

Jersey Lilly Saloon, **Ingomar**

You can drive right past Ingomar—a few breathing bodies short of being a ghost town—without a blink. Next time you're cruising the stretch of U.S. Highway 12 between Forsyth and Roundup, slow down when you see the sign for Ingomar, and turn off onto the short dirt road that takes you to the hitching posts at the Jersey Lilly Saloon, known internationally for its beans (more on them later). Set amid gently rolling plains, the Jersey Lilly hints that this was once a bustling town.

If you travel east from Roundup, you'll first pass Sumatra, a post-office-and-one-house town before coming upon the metropolis of Ingomar—population ten people and eight bison, which all together don't equal a crowd.

At its peak Ingomar was the world's largest sheep-shearing and wool shipping center, pumping out 2 million tons of wool a year. Shearing pens in Perth, Australia, used the Ingomar pens as a model. The Ingomar Hotel provided temporary lodging to the builders and buyers, the transients and railmen, the men and women and children who came to enjoy the Eden that was developing in the lush prairie grass of east-central Montana.

The Milwaukee Railroad was the primary link not only for shipping and receiving but also for water. The town had no potable water, so the railroad brought it in by water tender; it wasn't until the late 1980s that a water system was installed for the few remaining residents. This explains the lack of vegetation: water is too precious to waste on trees and gardens.

Between 1910 and 1920 the community grew to more than 2,500 residents. In addition to the bank and the Ingomar Hotel, the town's forty-plus businesses included lumberyards, saloons, blacksmith's shops, doctors, a general store—all the amenities you'd expect to find in any early 1900s boomtown. Depression and drought contributed to Ingomar's decline, along with fires—many of suspicious origin. The fires have destroyed a majority of the buildings over the years, a frequent consequence of economic depression. But it was the great fire of 1921 that ate away most of Ingomar. Although some businesses tried to rebuild, others opted to move elsewhere. But the Jersey Lilly stood.

Built in 1914 to house the upstart Wiley, Clark and Greening Bankers, the building officially became the First National Bank of Ingomar in 1921. That designation lasted for just six months, when the bank went into receivership after William Craig mishandled a portion of its funds. This forced the bank into its function as the Oasis Bar. Over the years it's hosted a variety of western folks—cowboys, railroaders, sheepherders, and pioneering entrepreneurs seeping into every pocket of growth in the expanding West.

Bill Seward was eighteen years old when his father, Bob, purchased the Oasis Bar in 1948 and renamed it the Jersey Lilly Saloon after Judge Roy Bean's bar in Langtry, Texas. Ten years later, Bill bought it from his dad. Today Jerry Brown owns the watering hole, which is still an oasis, a feel of the Old West in its wooden porch floorboards. It's a microcosm of the town. In the dingy walls, worn floors, and creaking doors of the Jersey Lilly, you can see and hear the history of Ingomar.

Inside you'll find the beans, actually more of a bean soup. The day we stopped in we were two of the two dozen or so patrons who were from as far away as Texas for the infamous legumes, the Texan having gone almost 100 miles out of his way to get there. Anna Maine, chief cook and bottle washer, served the beans in a saucepan, set on the table with bowls and hot sauce—we got two bowls each out of the order. In addition, we had two burgers, two beers, an order of fries, and an entire birthday cake (which got passed around)—total $11. Although locals find the Jersey Lilly inviting, the town and its saloon are inundated every year with tourists; many from Europe and the Orient have signed the guestbook.

Many places in the West have spent gobs of money trying to re-create the character that is the Jersey Lilly. While waiting for your food you can't help but notice the high, pressed-tin ceiling and massive hand-carved back bar; beer is stored in the old bank vault. Adding to the atmosphere is the original wooden phone booth in the corner and the pedestal sink behind the oversized screen door—each slam transporting you back in time.

After you've washed down the last bit of road dust, walk next door to the attached Community Organization shop for an impressive selection of hand-spun and hand-knitted woolen-wear and local crafts. The sweaters

With its planked walkway and hitching posts, the Jersey Lilly Saloon is not only the focal point of downtown Ingomar, it is downtown Ingomar.

are made of the finest Columbia sheep wool, but it's the process that makes them soft enough for even the most sensitive skin. Site of the original Bookman Store, the Community Organization uses its profits to maintain the former school gym that is now Ingomar's community center. The shop is open during tourist season only and caters to their dollars—an average sweater, for example, costs more than $100.

There's hardly a tree in sight, and you could swear that if you stood on the roof of the Jersey Lilly you'd be able to see Maryland on a clear day. The town lacks—besides people—the greenness of western Montana; what it has plenty of, though, is spirit, history, and some really great beans.

★ *Directions:*

In east-central Montana, northeast of Billings on U.S. Highway 12 between Roundup and Forsyth.

For more information:

406-358-2278; open seven days a week from 7 A.M. to 2 A.M.; closed Christmas Day, potluck supper on Thanksgiving Day.

Paddlefish, **Eastern Montana**

When someone mentions fishing in Montana you're likely to think of an Orvis vest–clad person waist deep in the middle of a rippling stream, snow-capped peaks in the background, leisurely casting for rainbow trout. After a brief tussle, the fish is pulled from the water and proudly held up for the world to see. But the scene is quite different in the eastern part of the state, where the quarry is the paddlefish. Here the fish seeker is most likely donned in a life vest and rubber boots, sporting mud-spattered khakis, the only scenery miles of flatland. Fishing is done from a boat or from shore, using saltwater gear and heavy sinkers (some people have even used spark plugs) that are more fit for a whale than for the dull brown, thick-skinned creature that when not feeding lies in the muck near the river bottom. Unlike the finesse required for trout fishing, muscles and a good back are needed to land this underwater denizen.

The paddlefish offers a real challenge and requires gobs of luck to catch, although catch is not the proper term—this fish does not take bait. Because it feeds on microscopic plankton, it needs to be snagged by jerking your line through the water. If you're lucky (and the fish isn't) you may hook one, but the real challenge begins when you try to haul it in. Weighing on average forty to fifty pounds, the paddler puts up a good fight, as would anyone with a treble hook stuck in them.

Polyodon spathula is a member of the sturgeon family, which has been around for 70 million years, and can live 30 years or more. With a look that only a mother could love, the Pinocchio of the fish world uses its two-foot-long snout to detect food as it sweeps through the murky water, but contrary to popular belief it isn't a bottom feeder, preferring instead to work mid-depth. Although the protuberance looks like it would make a formidable weapon, its main purpose is finding nutrition, but some contend it also helps its owner stay balanced while feeding.

Found in the Yellowstone and Missouri Rivers, these fish migrate upstream annually from Sakakawea Dam in North Dakota to spawn, as they have for years. Their populations in the rivers increased when in 1953 the Garrison Dam was closed; nine years later one was snagged in Montana, and the frenzy began. Fishermen swarmed to the site and pulled the hapless fish out in droves, so the Montana Department of Fish, Wildlife & Parks wisely established a limit, just as with big game, and the paddlefish is now carefully managed and listed as a species of special concern.

The fishing hot spot is Intake Diversion Dam about eighteen miles north of Glendive, where in May and June and sometimes into July this protected species becomes an industry all its own when fishermen gather to try for one of the 1,500 fish allowed by Fish, Wildlife & Parks. And you may keep what you catch regardless of size; the reasoning is that even the smallest paddler is at least ten to fifteen years old, so if it has come here to spawn it must be a mature fish. They weigh in between 14 and 100 pounds (females, from 55 to 60 pounds, outweigh the males by nearly two to one), although one lucky angler snagged a record $142\frac{1}{2}$-pounder. Take-home limit is one fish per person, but on two days each week you can catch and release under the watchful eye of FWP.

At Intake, interpretive signs tell you how to clean your prize. Most folks agree it's a bit tougher than walleye or trout but is pretty tasty and resembles lobster, whether batter dipped, deep fried, or boiled. You have to cut away the outer dark meat to get to the good stuff (only the inner white meat is edible) and there are no bones to deal with—the paddlefish has cartilage. But you do have to catch your own; it's illegal to sell it commercially and can't be found on any restaurant's menu. A license to snag one of these treasures will set back a resident $2.50 ($7.50 for out-of-staters) in addition to a $10 conservation license. Still, that's pretty fair eating for less than $1 a pound.

Glendive, "the paddlefish capital of the world," has benefited from this local fauna not only in drawing anglers to the area but by selling the roe. The chamber of commerce will clean your fish in exchange for the eggs (legally they can't charge for it), which they package and sell as caviar. At $30 and more a pound, it's a great fundraiser, with proceeds going to the community and toward paddlefish management.

But Glendive isn't the only town to recognize paddlefish potential. Not too far from the confluence of the Missouri and Yellowstone Rivers, Sidney kicks off the fishing season on May 1 with Peter Paddlefish Day. It began in 1983 as Montana's answer to Punxsutawney Phil when a few local gentlemen decided over their coffee cups that it would be a great

It takes two, Matt Golik, left, and Tom Anderson, right, to hold their catch. Photo courtesy of Missouri River Country.

idea to float a handmade paddlefish down the river to pay homage to their patron fish (the fabricated fish had to be on a boat because no one knew whether it would float). It didn't take long before residents decided Peter looked lonely, so Paula Paddlefish was added to the flotilla. Now an entire festival is built around these creatures, although Peter and Paula have been retired and no longer make the watery journey due to insurance liabilities. But the town still celebrates with a festival that includes the Paddlefish Run and Ride (a triathlon of sorts), barbecue, kite flying, and coloring contests. A costumed fish visits area schools to generate further interest (now there's a childhood memory that will stick with you through old age). Not that there's any lack of interest in these parts. Come May, it's just about all anyone talks about.

★ *Directions:*
Intake is midway between Sidney and Glendive on Montana Highway 16.

For more information:
Missouri River Country, 800-653-1319; Sidney Chamber of Commerce, 406-482-1916; Glendive Chamber of Commerce, 406-365-5601; Montana Department of Fish, Wildlife & Parks, 406-232-0900.

Testicle Festivals,
Ryegate *and* **Clinton**

Tired of the same old burger and fries? Maybe your palate needs to wake up with a Rocky Mountain oyster. Although hundreds of miles from any ocean, *these* oysters appear in spring and fall; in fact, entire festivals are geared around them—testicle festivals. So why are they called Rocky Mountain oysters? Well, if you were trying to get your kids to eat them, would you tell them what they really are?

Ever since there were cattle these delicacies have been removed from the business end of a bull or calf at spring branding; the castration cast-offs were tossed in buckets after the deed was done, to be fried or simply thrown on the campfire and downed at leisure (prairie oysters were once attached to sheep). The tradition of castrating helps ensure good breeding stock while growing meatier and tamer animals, but ranchers had more than they could use. One thing led to another and soon festivals popped up throughout the state. Although fests come and go, two in particular have been going for more than a decade—Ryegate Bar and Rock Creek Lodge. But that's where their similarity ends.

At Ryegate, $6.95 will get you all the nuts you can eat as well as roast pig and all the trimmings. On the second Saturday every June the festivities open with a traditional rodeo on Friday and a ranchers' rodeo on Saturday. The event has grown from a few locals with a gusto for glands to nearly 2,000, but even after 17 years it remains a family affair, something you wouldn't hesitate to take the kids to. Hay bales line the outdoor dance floor, better known as First Street the other 364 days of the year, where nut lovers dance until the wee hours.

Ask a handful of patrons what they taste like and you'll get a handful of different answers, but Rebecca Korell, bar employee and veteran nut fancier, claims they're chewy like chicken gizzards but taste more like thigh meat. "Last year we went through 200 pounds of nuts," she says, "but we had to resort to buying them commercially—there just aren't enough ranchers to supply us." Actually, nearly every festival relies on meat processors for their supply since ranching has gone modern and uses rubber bands instead of the labor-intensive, knife-wielding cowboy. "Most of us like local nuts better than imports but a newcomer won't know the difference," Rebecca says. And newcomers show up in droves from all over the country; many, like one couple from Australia, plan their vacation around test fests.

Ryegate's boast of no fights in the past two years is lost on Rock Creek. If you go to this testy festy you may want to leave the kids at home—these people party hearty. In 1999 it billed itself as the last best party of the millennium, and who could argue when the featured attraction was the Seattle Cossacks Motorcycle Stunt and Drill Team. But every September, wet T-shirt (shirt optional) and hairy chest contests rule. Revelers are invited to sit on the bar's amply endowed wooden bull (again, shirt optional) to help wind down the ball.

If you can't fit festival weekend into your schedule, you can still get a taste of the bar's ambiance—from the 1,444 baseball caps and various college and pro football helmets attached to the ceiling to the massive photo album that showcases past partiers. Its huge gift shop offers, among the hundreds of items, patches, mugs, beer can holders, caps, T-shirts, and even panties, all emblazoned with festival slogans. For every souvenir there's a pun to go with it: No Nuts No Glory, Have a Ball, Sometimes You Feel Like a Nut, That's No Bull, the list goes on.

If you're unlucky enough to miss both festivals, take heart, many restaurants around the state serve them year-round but with much less fanfare. And, you never know when your favorite bar is going to host its own festival. Either way, you'll have a ball. In fact, that very slogan is what encouraged one college grad to move to Montana. Off to find his place in the world he couldn't decide on Idaho, Washington, or Montana, but when he saw the brochure touting a testicle festival, of all things, he decided that this was where he wanted to put down roots. Not that he wanted to attend one, he just liked Montana's attitude. The department of tourism would be so proud.

★ *Directions:*
Ryegate Bar is on U.S. Highway 12, 60 miles northwest of Billings; Rock Creek Lodge is in Clinton off Interstate 90, 20 miles east of Missoula.

For more information:
Ryegate, always the second Saturday in June, 406-568-2330; Rock Creek, always September, 406-825-4868, www.testyfesty.com.

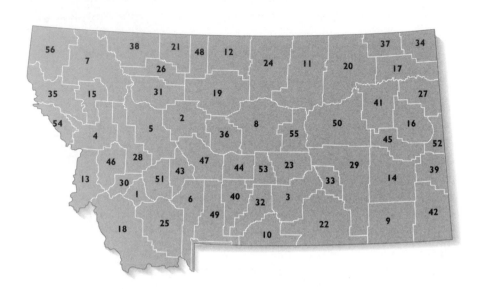

License Plates—did you know . . .

Montana's license plates have a secret code that's easy to crack. Once you know it you'll be able to figure out what part of the state the car is from. The first number on each plate designates its county, which is numbered from 1 as the largest to 56, the smallest, based on population. But things have changed since the system began and the ranking is no longer accurate. For example, Billings at number 3 has grown to take over the number 1 spot, and as a result there is a grassroots movement under way to make the plates geographically correct. As it stands, a prefix of 3P means that car was registered in Yellowstone County (which includes Billings) as a passenger (P) vehicle; a 3T means it's a truck. The P has been eliminated on the new plates.

Montana seems to have a larger than normal number of vanity plates, but even these usually have a small number to identify the county of origin.

Number	County	County Seat
1	Silverbow	Butte
2	Cascade	Great Falls
3	Yellowstone	Billings
4	Missoula	Missoula
5	Lewis and Clark	Helena
6	Gallatin	Bozeman
7	Flathead	Kalispell
8	Fergus	Lewistown
9	Powder River	Broadus
10	Carbon	Red Lodge
11	Phillips	Malta
12	Hill	Havre
13	Ravalli	Hamilton
14	Custer	Miles City
15	Lake	Polson

16	Dawson	Glendive
17	Roosevelt	Wolf Point
18	Beaverhead	Dillon
19	Chouteau	Fort Benton
20	Valley	Glasgow
21	Toole	Shelby
22	Big Horn	Hardin
23	Musselshell	Roundup
24	Blaine	Chinook
25	Madison	Virginia City
26	Pondera	Conrad
27	Richland	Sidney
28	Powell	Deer Lodge
29	Rosebud	Forsyth
30	Deer Lodge	Anaconda
31	Teton	Choteau
32	Stillwater	Columbus
33	Treasure	Hysham
34	Sheridan	Plentywood
35	Sanders	Thompson Falls
36	Judith Basin	Stanford
37	Daniels	Scobey
38	Glacier	Cut Bank
39	Fallon	Baker
40	Sweet Grass	Big Timber
41	McCone	Circle
42	Carter	Ekalaka
43	Broadwater	Townsend
44	Wheatland	Harlowton
45	Prairie	Terry
46	Granite	Philipsburg
47	Meagher	White Sulphur Springs
48	Liberty	Chester
49	Park	Livingston
50	Garfield	Jordan
51	Jefferson	Boulder
52	Wibaux	Wibaux
53	Golden Valley	Ryegate
54	Mineral	Superior
55	Petroleum	Winnett
56	Lincoln	Libby

Index

About *the* **Authors**

John and Durrae Johanek start out all their trips from Bozeman. When they're not exploring the four corners of the state they have real jobs. To keep the family car's gas tank topped off, John is a magazine design consultant and partner in Ayers/Johanek Publication Design, Inc. He also writes a regular design column for *Editors Only* and is a frequent contributor to *Folio* and other publishing trade magazines.

Durrae keeps herself occupied by working eight days a week as an editorial freelancer. She lives with her four cats, two goats, and John, not necessarily in that order. She has a B.A. in English from Kutztown University of Pennsylvania and has written several nature-related magazine articles appearing in *Bird Watcher's Digest* and *Popular Mechanics*.

Their appetite for Montana is as big as the state itself. They enjoy birding, wildlife watching, and cross-country skiing. Whenever they can, they take to the back roads in search of all three, and even a gumbo road or two.

It Happened in *Series from TwoDot™ Books*

An imprint of Falcon Publishing

TWODOT™

Featured in this series are fascinating stories about events that helped shape each state's history. Written in a lively, easy-to-read style, each book features 31-34 stories for history buffs of all ages. Entertaining and informative, each book is 6x9" and features b&w illustrations.

It Happened in Arizona
It Happened in Colorado
It Happened in Georgia
It Happened in Massachusetts
It Happened in Montana
It Happened in New Mexico
It Happened in New York
It Happened in North Carolina
It Happened in Northern California
It Happened in Oregon
It Happened in Southern California
It Happened in Texas
It Happened in Utah
It Happened in Washington

More from TwoDot™ Books

Bozeman and the Gallatin Valley
Charlie's Trail: The Life and Art of C.M. Russell
Flight of the Dove: The Story of Jeannette Rankin
Growing up Western
Heart of the Trail: The Stories of Eight Wagon Train Women
Jeannette Rankin: Bright Star in the Big Sky
Men with Sand: Great Explorers of the American West
Montana Campfire Tales: Fourteen Historical Essays
More Than Petticoats: Remarkable Montana Women
More Than Petticoats: Remarkable Oregon Women
More Than Petticoats: Remarkable Tennessee Women
More Than Petticoats: Remarkable Washington Women
The Champion Buffalo Hunter
The Only Good Bear is a Dead Bear
Today I Baled Some Hay to Feed the Sheep the Coyotes Eat

The TwoDot line features classic western literature and history. Each book celebrates and interprets the vast spaces and rich culture of the American West.

FALCON®

To order check with your local bookseller or call Falcon® at
1-800-582-2665
Ask for a FREE catalog featuring a complete list of titles on nature, outdoor recreation, travel and regional history.
www.falcon.com

More than Petticoats series

With in-depth and accurate coverage, this series pays tribute to the often unheralded efforts and achievements of the women who settled the West. Each title in the series includes a collection of absorbing biographies and b&w historical photos.

TWODOT

An Imprint of Falcon Publishing

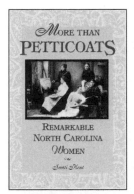  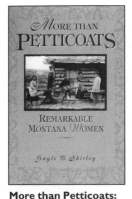

More than Petticoats: Remarkable North Carolina Women
by Scotti Kent
$12.95
ISBN 1-56044-900-4

More than Petticoats: Remarkable California Women
by Erin H. Turner
$9.95
ISBN 1-56044-859-8

More than Petticoats: Remarkable Montana Women
by Gayle C. Shirley
$8.95
ISBN 1-56044-363-4

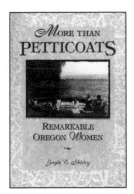 

More than Petticoats: Remarkable Oregon Women
by Gayle C. Shirley
$9.95
ISBN 1-56044-668-4

More than Petticoats: Remarkable Washington Women
by L.E. Bragg
$9.95
ISBN 1-56044-667-6

TwoDot™ features books that celebrate and interpret the rich culture and history of regional America.

To order check with your local bookseller or call Falcon® at **1-800-582-2665.**
Ask for a FREE catalog featuring a complete list of titles on nature, outdoor recreation, travel and regional history.

www.falcon.com

FALCON®

FALCON GUIDES ® Leading the way™

FalconGuides® are available for where-to-go hiking, mountain biking, rock climbing, walking, scenic driving, fishing, rockhounding, paddling, birding, wildlife viewing, and camping. We also have FalconGuides on essential outdoor skills and subjects and field identification. The following titles are currently available, but this list grows every year. For a free catalog with a complete list of titles, call FALCON toll-free at 1-800-582-2665.

BIRDING GUIDES

Birding Georgia
Birding Illinois
Birding Minnesota
Birding Montana
Birding Northern California
Birding Texas
Birding Utah

PADDLING GUIDES

Paddling Minnesota
Paddling Montana
Paddling Okefenokee
Paddling Oregon
Paddling Yellowstone & Grand
    Teton National Parks

WALKING

Walking Colorado Springs
Walking Denver
Walking Portland
Walking Seattle
Walking St. Louis
Walking San Francisco
Walking Virginia Beach

CAMPING GUIDES

Camping Arizona
Camping California's
    National Forests
Camping Colorado
Camping Oregon
Camping Southern California
Camping Washington
Recreation Guide to Washington
    National Forests

FIELD GUIDES

Bitterroot: Montana State Flower
Canyon Country Wildflowers
Central Rocky Mountain
    Wildflowers
Chihuahuan Desert Wildflowers
Great Lakes Berry Book
New England Berry Book
Ozark Wildflowers
Pacific Northwest Berry Book
Plants of Arizona
Rare Plants of Colorado
Rocky Mountain Berry Book
Scats & Tracks of the Pacific
    Coast States
Scats & Tracks of the Rocky Mtns.
Sierra Nevada Wildflowers
Southern Rocky Mountain
    Wildflowers
Tallgrass Prairie Wildflowers
Western Trees

ROCKHOUNDING GUIDES

Rockhounding Arizona
Rockhounding California
Rockhounding Colorado
Rockhounding Montana
Rockhounding Nevada
Rockhounding New Mexico
Rockhounding Texas
Rockhounding Utah
Rockhounding Wyoming

HOW-TO GUIDES

Avalanche Aware
Backpacking Tips
Bear Aware
Desert Hiking Tips
Hiking with Dogs
Hiking with Kids
Mountain Lion Alert
Reading Weather
Route Finding
Using GPS
Wild Country Companion
Wilderness First Aid
Wilderness Survival

MORE GUIDEBOOKS

Backcountry Horseman's
    Guide to Washington
Family Fun in Montana
Family Fun in Yellowstone
Exploring Canyonlands & Arches
    National Parks
Exploring Hawaii's Parklands
Exploring Mount Helena
Exploring Southern California
    Beaches
Hiking Hot Springs of the Pacific
    Northwest
Touring Arizona Hot Springs
Touring California & Nevada
    Hot Springs
Touring Colorado Hot Springs
Touring Montana and Wyoming
    Hot Springs
Trail Riding Western Montana
Wilderness Directory
Wild Montana
Wild Utah
Wild Virginia

■ *To order any of these books, check with your local bookseller*
or call FALCON ® at **1-800-582-2665**.
Visit us on the world wide web at:
www.Falcon.com

FALCON®

FALCONGUIDES ® Leading the Way™

---

www.Falcon.com

Since 1979, Falcon® has brought you the best in outdoor recreational guidebooks. Now you can access that same reliable and accurate information online.

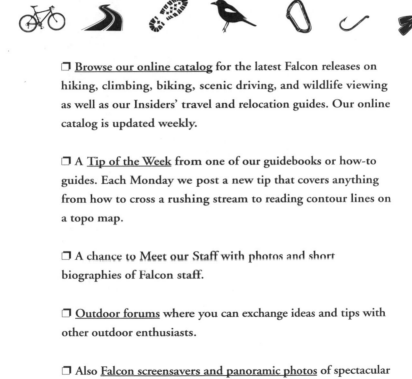

❒ <u>Browse our online catalog</u> for the latest Falcon releases on hiking, climbing, biking, scenic driving, and wildlife viewing as well as our Insiders' travel and relocation guides. Our online catalog is updated weekly.

❒ A <u>Tip of the Week</u> from one of our guidebooks or how-to guides. Each Monday we post a new tip that covers anything from how to cross a rushing stream to reading contour lines on a topo map.

❒ A chance to <u>Meet our Staff</u> with photos and short biographies of Falcon staff.

❒ <u>Outdoor forums</u> where you can exchange ideas and tips with other outdoor enthusiasts.

❒ Also <u>Falcon screensavers and panoramic photos</u> of spectacular destinations.

And much more!

Plan your next outdoor adventure at our web site. Point your browser to www.Falcon.com and get FalconGuided!

FALCON®

Charles M. Russell

TWODOT®

Charles M. Russell, Legacy
By Larry Len Peterson
Co-published with the
C. M. Russell Museum.

$95.00 cloth binding
456 pp

**The C. M. Russell
Postcard Book**
Co-published with the
C. M. Russell Museum.

$8.95 sc
22 color postcards

Charlie's Trail
The Life and Art
of C. M. Russell
By Gayle C. Shirley
Co-published with the
C. M. Russell Museum.

$10.95 sc
72 pp

MONTANA
HISTORICAL
SOCIETY
PRESS

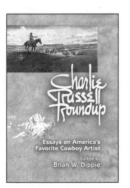

**Charlie Russell
Roundup**
Essays on America's
Favorite Cowboy Artist
*Edited and with an
introduction by
Brian W. Dippie*

$39.95 hc $19.95 sc
356 pp

**Charlie Russell
Journal**

$12.95 hc
128 pp

To order, check with your local bookseller or call Falcon at 1-800-582-2665.
*Ask for a FREE catalog featuring a complete list of titles on
nature, outdoor recreation, travel, and the West.*

www.falcon.com

FALCON®